➤— For Bob ⟶

with googols of love

GHOSTLY

CAMPFIRE STORIES

OF WESTERN CANADA

GHOSTLY
CAMPFIRE STORIES
—OF WESTERN CANADA→

Barbara Smith

HERITAGE

VICTORIA
VANCOUVER
CALGARY

Heritage House Publishing Company Ltd.
heritagehouse.ca

CATALOGUING INFORMATION AVAILABLE FROM LIBRARY AND ARCHIVES CANADA

978-1-77203-245-1 (pbk)
978-1-77203-246-8 (epub)

Edited by Karla Decker
Proofread by Jesmine Cham
Cover and interior design by Jacqui Thomas
Cover illustration by Mark R/shutterstock.com and Jacqui Thomas

The interior of this book was produced on 100% post-consumer recycled paper, processed chlorine free, and printed with vegetable-based inks.

We acknowledge the financial support of the Government of Canada through the Canada Book Fund (CBF) and the Canada Council for the Arts, and the Province of British Columbia through the British Columbia Arts Council and the Book Publishing Tax Credit.

22 21 20 19 18 1 2 3 4 5

Printed in Canada

 # CONTENTS

INTRODUCTION

Hello, happy campers!

Thank you for inviting me to your campfires again this year. Please pass the marshmallows. Don't ask me to sing, though—not even old camping songs. I'm a really, really bad singer, but I do know how to tell a spooky story or two—or two dozen, in fact, in this book. Well, there are actually twenty-five new campfire tales here in my sequel to *Campfire Stories of Western Canada*. The last story's a bonus, like an extra track of music—if I could sing, that is.

Just for a little added *frisson*, not all of the stories in this collection are strictly fiction. Some are based on actual events documented in newspapers and police reports. You see, I'm a big fan of *true* creepy stories. To me, they're even scarier than fictional ones because the truth often comes to us as mere fragments of a story, leaving our imaginations to fill in the mysterious missing details. If you're interested in learning which tales are completely made up and which ones are dramatized accounts of actual events, just check the Afterword—which, logically, is at the back of the book.

You'll find camping spots in all four Western Canadian provinces represented here. Some stories aren't tightly tied to a specific location, so if you find one that you think your fellow campers will enjoy, feel free to adapt the setting in whatever way you wish. Of course, that means you have to know the story pretty well before you pack the book away in your camping gear, so do read it over to yourself a few times before you go live, so to speak.

Even if you choose to read from the book rather than tell the story yourself, be sure to go over it a few times before the group settles in. Think of yourself as an actor performing a short play. Make sure each word you speak is clear, and emphasize your performance by changing your voice tone, adding gestures, and even pausing now and then to create suspense. And don't forget to look up at your audience every now and then so that they feel completely included in the spine-tingling experience.

Summers only last so long in Western Canada, but that doesn't mean we can't tell campfire stories all year long. All you have to do is gather a group of friends together, dim the lights and let the stories begin. Of course, you can also enjoy reading them by yourself. If you get too scared, just be brave, little camper, and try to remember that not *all* of the stories in this book are true!

Happy tales to you!

THE SCREAMS

Many years ago, in central Alberta, there was a town so small that it wasn't really a town, just a sleepy village that got a bit livelier in the summer. The gas station had been gone for years, but at least there was still a general store. The folks who came to camp nearby did all their shopping at that general store—although the place creeped most of them out and everyone was just a little bit afraid of Anita Frey, the woman who ran the store. Even the most polite campers agreed that Anita was wound a bit tight, to say the least. Little did those holidayers know that they had every right to be spooked by the store, and they certainly couldn't have known of the horrors that poor Mrs. Frey suffered day after day after day—or rather, night after night.

Every evening at closing time, after she had locked the front door, Mrs. Frey made her way to the back of the store and the tiny room she called home. She would fix herself a simple supper and brew a strong mug of tea. Then she would sit by the fireplace and wait. She never had to wait very long for the blood-curdling, disembodied screams that echoed from nowhere and everywhere. They were as predictable as the setting sun.

She would hold her hands over her ears, and then, when that didn't help, she'd take to her bed and bury her head under pillows and blankets. But nothing blocked out the ghostly wailing.

The years came and went until the summer when campers arrived to find the store locked. Anita Frey was nowhere to be found. The partners from the city who owned the building tried to entice new proprietors to the business, but none lasted more than a few weeks; some only stayed a few days, and one did not even linger through the first night.

Soon, stories leaked out to the surrounding community—stories about the place being haunted by unearthly shrieks. Eventually, the owners gave up on the business and sent a demolition crew to tear down the dilapidated old building.

The crew's foreman was sure the job wouldn't take very long. The place was mostly rotting lumber, save for the huge fireplace in the tiny room at the back. They'd need to tackle that brute stone by stone, starting from the top of the chimney.

As the foreman had expected, that part of the demolition was slow, heavy work. Men stood on a scaffold chipping away at the mortar that had held the chimney blocks together for longer than anyone could remember. The other workers cleared away the debris when it was safe to do so.

Finally, the chimney was nothing more than a pile of rocks near the foreman's pickup truck.

With the chimney down, all that was left to demolish was the fireplace itself. "Two of you can work on that," the foreman instructed. "One on either side. That'll get it done twice as fast so we can get back to the city before nightfall."

The two labourers swung their sledgehammers rhythmically, and soon the fireplace was not much more than a hearth.

"Can we leave it like this?" one of the men asked, pointing to the bottom few layers of stone.

"No, we can't, but you two take a break while I get this stuff cleared away," the foreman instructed. "There's not much left to do after that."

Soon, the two men were back at it, but one had only taken a couple of swings before he stopped, his hammer poised over his head. "What the . . . ?"

There, lying behind the foundation stones, was a human skull, its empty eye sockets gaping and its open jaw locked in mid-scream. All these years, a body—or at least part of one—had lain buried under that fireplace. At long last, the mystery of the ghostly screams had been solved.

The workers composed themselves as best they could before digging a small hole a few metres away and carefully placing the skull in it. Then they covered the tiny grave with dusty soil. Each man said a few words after the burial. Most of them simply wished that the soul who had once inhabited that skull would now rest in peace.

No one wondered any longer where those phantom shrieks had come from, nor why it was that poor Anita Frey was always agitated and had finally fled from the haunted store.

THE VISITOR

Petra sat at the edge of the group of campers huddled around a roaring bonfire. There were easily twenty-five people there by now. Mario, Petra's cousin, was hosting the get-together at his parents' cabin on Clear Lake, in Manitoba's Riding Mountain National Park. Even though they were first cousins, Mario and Petra had never met before. Their fathers were brothers who'd had a falling out years before and hadn't spoken to one another since. Mario had stumbled across Petra's Facebook page a little more than a year before, and the two young people had been in touch since then. *You'd think our fathers could've buried the hatchet long enough to tell each other that their children were born,* Petra thought, but she knew better than to mention anything at home. No one but the two fathers knew what had caused the grudge, and the rift was apparently permanent.

Despite that, Mario and Petra had enjoyed their friendship on Facebook for more than a year when they decided they should meet in person.

"Come to Winnipeg," Mario urged. "We'll spend a few days at the lake."

And so it was that Petra boarded a plane in Calgary, telling her parents that she'd be staying with friends in Manitoba and that she'd keep her phone on all the time she was gone.

To help celebrate Petra's trip to Manitoba, Mario had invited some of his friends to the cottage for the weekend. Everyone said how great it was that the next generation of the family wasn't carrying on the feud.

Petra had instantly fallen in love with the quaint old cottage, with its exposed log walls and braided rugs scattered about on the floors of all the rooms. There would be lots of people staying overnight, and she had been assigned a top bunk in one of the three tiny bedrooms. Even that tickled her fancy. Growing up as an only child, she had never shared a bedroom with anyone and had certainly never slept in a bunk bed.

All of Mario's friends had been warm and welcoming to her. They'd spent the day paddleboarding, swimming, playing beach volleyball, and eating far too many barbecued hot dogs and hamburgers. Late in the evening, after they'd all gathered around a well-stoked beach fire singing songs, Mario announced that they'd run out of his secret ingredient for s'mores (chocolate sprinkles!) but by then, Petra was ready to call it a night. She looked around the group. People had broken off into clusters and were chatting quietly. Even the fellow who'd been playing the guitar and leading an earlier singsong had stopped playing and was deep in a conversation with the pretty girl beside him.

Quietly, Petra got to her feet, brushed the sand off the back of her shorts and walked toward the cabin. She was sure she'd be asleep before any of the others made their way from the beach. The old screen door creaked as she opened and closed it. For some reason, that simple noise brought a smile to her face. *Perhaps that's why cabins and cottages are so much more fun than regular houses in the city,* she thought. *At the lake, no one worries about perfection. Everyone's having too much fun to be bothered oiling a creaky hinge.*

The dark stillness inside the cottage was so soothing that Petra decided to make herself a cup of tea and read for a while before going to bed. Humming an old campfire song, she turned to take a mug from the cupboard.

And that's when she saw him: a man leaning against the kitchen doorway.

"Oh!" she exclaimed.

The man smiled.

"I'm sorry, I thought I was alone."

"It's all right," the stranger assured her. "You are alone— well, pretty much anyway."

That was a strange comment, Petra thought and gave a brittle, nervous laugh. Was she safe in here with him? Perhaps she should let him know her connection to the cottage. "I'm visiting from Calgary. My uncle and his wife own the cabin. My cousin— their son, I mean—he's still down at the beach with the others."

The man nodded. "I should have introduced myself. I'm Joseph."

"I'm Petra," she said, shaking his outstretched hand. "I was just about to make some tea. Would you like a cup? Your hands are cold."

"No, thanks," he replied. "But the living room's nice and warm. I'll happily sit with you and visit while you're having tea."

Petra smiled. She liked Joseph's manners. He was kind of old-fashioned. He had beautiful blue eyes, and his black hair was slicked back. *He's either just gone for a swim and his hair's still wet, or he has some kind of gel in his hair. Maybe he considers himself a metro-sexual or something*, she thought.

Joseph started the conversation by explaining that he always found families fascinating and asked Petra to tell him about herself. "Only if you're comfortable, of course," he added.

The two sat at opposite ends of an old wicker sofa. Petra switched on a nearby lamp. The cushions were lumpy with age, so she put her back on the arm of the couch and swung her bare feet up. Hugging her knees to her chest, she considered the stranger's question. She stole a look at him. He was definitely very handsome, but he had a different look about him, not one she'd ever seen before. She certainly didn't feel afraid of him. Besides, all those people around the campfire were no more than fifty metres away. Now that she could see him in the light, she noticed that he wasn't much older than she was. His offer to keep her company had seemed a bit odd, but maybe he was just one of those people who was endlessly interested in people.

"I live in Calgary, still with my parents because I'm a student. I'm in nursing, another year and a half to go," she explained. "How about you?"

The handsome young man shrugged. "Maybe the reason I like hearing about other people's lives is that honestly, I don't have much of a life myself."

"Oh, that can't be true!"

Petra's words were interrupted by the group from the campfire trooping into the house.

"Hello! We're in here," Petra called out.

"Hey, cousin," replied Mario. "I didn't know you'd come up to the cabin."

"Uh-huh," she said. "Joseph and I have been getting to know one another."

"Okay . . . " Mario replied a little hesitantly.

Petra turned back to acknowledge Joseph, but he was nowhere to be seen.

"He must've gone back outside."

"Okay . . . " Mario repeated, still making those two syllables sound hesitant, as if what she'd said was not okay at all. Then his face brightened, and he announced, "Well, tomorrow's another day. I think we should all hit the hay."

Petra happily climbed the ladder to her cozy bed and slept a deep, dreamless sleep until she heard people stirring in the cabin's kitchen the next morning.

"Can I help with anything?" she inquired.

"No, but you're the last one up, so you get stuck with the dishes," Mario told her with a good-natured smile. "For now, just find a place at the table."

Petra did as she was told and was looking around for Joseph when Mario brought her a huge plate of bacon, eggs, and home fries. "Looks delicious, thanks," she said.

Twenty minutes later, she was alone in the cabin once again. *I wonder where Joseph disappeared to last night?* Petra wondered. *Oh well, maybe I'll see him again this morning.*

Once she had dried the last dish and put it away, Petra went into the living room and tidied up from the night before. There were old family pictures in frames above the fireplace. She loved black-and-white photos and examined each one carefully. There were several group shots of people in front of this cabin. She could tell which ones were the oldest by the height of the trees by the door. And then there was a smaller frame. The picture it held was formally posed, a head-and-shoulders shot of a young man wearing an old-fashioned soldier's uniform. Petra picked up the frame and angled it toward the light from the picture window.

"That's Joseph!" she exclaimed out loud to the empty room. "I was right. He is handsome. I wonder who he is."

"Come on, slowpoke!" Mario called in through the screen door.

"Okay, I'll be right there. But first, could you come in here for a minute? I want to ask you something."

Mario came in and saw that she was holding a photograph from the mantel. "Which one do you have there?"

Petra turned the frame toward her cousin. Mario was quiet for a moment. "That's Uncle Joe. He was my mother's brother. He enlisted during the Second World War, but he didn't make it back. Losing him nearly killed my grandparents, I can tell you."

"Joe?" Petra questioned.

"Yeah, that was what they called him—short for Joseph, of course."

Petra swallowed.

"Come on," Mario urged. "There's a vicious game of horseshoes starting out on the back lawn, and I need you on my team."

"Okay," Petra said quietly. "I'll be out soon. I just need a moment."

"You okay?" he asked.

"I will be, I promise. For now, though, I just need some time."

"Are you sure? You're awfully pale. You look as though you've seen a ghost."

Petra nodded, realizing that was exactly what had happened.

THE GRAVEYARD
OF THE PACIFIC

PROLOGUE *Sailors are a superstitious lot. They'll tell you that it's bad luck to start a voyage on a Friday and that changing the name of a ship will bring ill fortune, but the most feared of all omens is seeing a phantom ship—the image of a vessel still plying the world's waterways years, even centuries, after it has sunk. Unfortunately, sightings of phantom ships are frequent enough that there is even a name for them. Such a vessel is called a* Flying Dutchman, *in honour of the first recorded phantom ship. That ship was sailing around the Horn of Africa, whereas the ship in this story came to its demise just off the west coast of Vancouver Island.*

Troy and Mark had been friends for years. Both were athletes and loved sports, but other than that, their interests were as different as could be. Through high school, Troy had excelled in everything to do with science, while Mark had an easy time learning languages. After they graduated, they spent their gap year working side by side at a store in Winnipeg's North End. Come September, though, their easy togetherness would end because they were going off to universities on nearly opposite sides of Canada.

"Let's do something mind-boggling before we leave for school," Troy suggested one afternoon in early August.

"Like what?" Mark asked.

"Well, we're both in good shape, so why not try hiking the West Coast Trail? It's on the west side of Vancouver Island."

Mark glared at Troy. "I know where it is, man, but are you crazy? I've heard that hike's insane."

"Exactly. That's why we should do it," Troy countered, offering his friend a fist bump.

And so it was that a few weeks later, the two young men packed up every bit of hiking gear they owned and flew to Victoria, British Columbia's capital, on the southern tip of Vancouver Island. From there they made their way west to the town of Port Renfrew to start their adventure.

"I can't believe we're doing this!" Troy could barely contain his enthusiasm as they started out the next morning.

Mark nodded, mutely wondering how he had been talked into doing this hike. Once he saw the rugged scenery and amazing views from the trail, though, he was sold. By the time they made camp at the end of the first day, they were exhausted but exhilarated.

"Hey, I know an old ghost story from around here," Mark said.

Troy snorted sarcastically.

"Yeah, really. There's a pub near Port Renfrew that's supposed to be haunted by the ghost of the original owner. Do you want to hear the story? It's pretty creepy."

The only reply to Mark's question was the sound of snoring from the sleeping bag next to his, so he settled in for the night too. Tomorrow would be another long day of strenuous hiking.

By day three of the hike, the two young men were thoroughly fatigued and lingered at the camp they'd made, but the following day, completely revived, they were off again, full of enthusiasm and energy for the last days of their adventure.

It was twilight on the sixth day as they approached the northernmost point of the trail. They agreed that the trip had indeed been a once-in-a-lifetime adventure.

"Pachena Point's just up ahead. Want to camp here for the last night?" Troy asked.

"It's only another few kilometres to Bamfield. We could spend the night in a comfortable hotel there instead."

"What? And miss one more night under the stars? I think not," Troy said. "Besides, you've never told me that ghost story you were talking about."

"New rules. I'm not going to tell the ghost story till we get to sleep in proper beds. And just for the record, there aren't any stars out tonight. It's totally cloudy."

"You sound like an old lady," Troy said teasingly before rolling over and going to sleep.

Mark tried to do the same, but he couldn't relax. His mind was racing, he was restless, and he had an uncomfortable feeling that something was just not quite right. "Maybe I'm more tired than I thought," he muttered to himself under his breath.

He sat up and looked out across the darkening sky and the calm water below. He had to admit that the hike had been everything Troy promised. Canada's western coastline was definitely a sight to behold. *Better breathe this all in before we head back to the prairies*, he thought. *Too bad it's overcast tonight, but the air is fabulous. It even has that electrically charged tang to it, like there's going to be a thunderstorm.*

Just as Mark was about to lie down again, he noticed a small bright spot on the horizon. He looked again. A patch of light hovered out there just above the horizon. Was it mist? It must be mist—but a bright, white mist. He'd never seen anything like it before. As he watched, the cloud of mist thickened and began to glow, and there was something inside the mist. A moment later, the cloud brightened even more, and Mark could clearly make out a shape inside. It was an old-fashioned ship that appeared to be battling heavy winds and enormous waves.

"What the . . . ?"

Mark reached down to shake Troy awake but then thought better of it. *What if I'm so tired that I'm seeing things? He'll never let me live it down. This can't really be happening. Must be my imagination.*

But the ship was really there: an old-fashioned ship battling strong winds and enormous waves, all encompassed in a brilliant white cloud of mist. The vision was so clear that Mark could see people clambering up the ship's rigging to get as far above the deadly waves as they could. There were women clutching children, hanging on for their lives. They seemed to be screaming in fear, but no sounds escaped from the cloud. The details of the scene were distinct enough that he could make out the name printed on the ship's bow: *Valencia.*

Mark's mind raced. *This can't really be happening. Am I asleep? Is this all a dream?* He shook his head and pinched his arm as he watched the silent tableau play out before his eyes. Wind and rain battered the beleaguered ship, and waves swamped the deck. Men working along both the port and starboard sides of the vessel fought to launch lifeboats as people struggled across the lurching deck toward the small boats, their only hope of survival.

A huge wave slammed across the ship's bow. Mark's heart pounded in his chest. *That must have washed people overboard. At least the passengers in the lifeboats will be safe.*

But they weren't. Horrified, Mark watched as the first two lifeboats flipped over as they were being lowered, throwing every soul to a dreadful death. A third lifeboat made it to the surface of the churning water before capsizing. Mark felt sick. *People are drowning by the dozens. Please let me be dreaming. I can't watch this much longer!*

Then, slowly, the bright white mist and the ghastly vision enshrouded within it began to break apart into mere flickers of light before fading away. Within seconds, there was no longer a cloud of mist and certainly no sinking ship with passengers fleeing.

It must've been a dream, Mark told himself again and lay down with his sleeping bag pulled over his head. The next thing he knew, Troy was shaking him awake. Mark felt terrible, as if he had the worst case of flu ever. And that dream—that was no mere dream. That was a nightmare! There was no way he was going to tell Troy. They only had a few more kilometres to hike, and they would have accomplished their goal of hiking the West Coast Trail. *Just in time, before this trail drives me completely crazy*, Mark thought.

The two friends broke camp while munching on granola bars for breakfast. They helped each other hoist their backpacks into place and headed toward the last section of the trail. Mark lagged behind Troy because he kept looking back at the sea where he'd seen—or thought he'd seen—the strange drama playing out before him.

"Keep up!" Troy called back.

Mark took one last look out over the water. There was nothing unusual, not so much as a sign that there ever had been anything unusual, certainly not a foundering ship in a cloud of bright white mist. *I guess I'll never know exactly what it was I saw last night,* he thought, turning back to the trail. He drew in a couple of deep breaths to clear his head. There was that electrified tang in the air again. *Could it just be the smell of the sea,* he wondered before turning to follow Troy on the path.

Mark had only taken a few steps when he heard a rustling in the grass beside the trail. A snake? Mark hated snakes. He quickened his step, but the rustling kept pace with him. Then he saw the tops of the bushes at the side of the path move. This was no snake. It was a person: a wet and dishevelled-looking man gestured at Mark to come to him. The man's body shimmered as if it was made of billions of tiny, bright specks of white. His voice cracked like an old radio report as he spoke. "Wait! Don't walk away from me. I need help. Our ship was tossed against the reef in the storm."

Mark was too startled to move. The air was sharp and unnaturally chilly. *This guy has to be from that ship I saw last night. But it wasn't real. It couldn't have been. It was a mirage, and so is he.*

The cracking voice spoke again. "You must go for help. A few of us made it to shore, but the waves were so bad that most of those poor devils were washed back into the sea, God rest their souls. I might be the only one alive, but I've got to get help in case there are others."

I've lost it completely, Mark thought as he gulped in as much air as his fear-filled body would allow. *I'm just going to keep walking till I catch up with Troy. If this guy's real, then he can follow me. If he's not real, I'll get my head examined as soon as I get home.*

The apparition kept talking. "My friend went overboard. He was the one who talked me into signing on with that boat in the first place. We hadn't worked for weeks. We were staying at the Valencia Street Hotel in San Francisco. He said this ship would bring us luck because she was called the *Valencia*, like the hotel."

Mark stumbled forward. "Guess your friend was dead wrong, eh?" he said, wondering if he was talking to himself. But there was no answer. He looked around. The trail was empty. The man had simply vanished. No one was there. The biting, acrid scent in the air was gone. Mark hurried to catch up to Troy. He would be so glad when this trip was over.

When they reached Bamfield, the relief was almost too much. Mark had no energy left at all. They found a place to get a hot meal, and he let Troy do most of the talking. The restaurant was busy, so they had to ask to share a table with a fellow wearing a Parks Canada uniform.

"Sure, you can join me," the man said. "You two look like you survived the West Coast Trail."

"We did indeed," said Troy.

Mark took a sip of coffee. "You know this area well then, do you?"

"As well as anyone, I guess."

"Do you know if there were ever any shipwrecks off Pachena Point?"

"Shipwrecks? Yes, absolutely. The part of the trail you just hiked used to be called the Dominion Lifesaving Trail. It was put in way back in 1907 so shipwreck survivors could get to help. It must've been some job laying out that first path in the wilderness, but it had to be done."

"Why's that?"

"Well, the final straw was the wreck of the *Valencia*. She ran aground in January 1906. Nearly 150 people drowned; there were very few survivors. It's still considered the worst shipwreck on the West Coast in terms of lives lost. Those waters aren't called the graveyard of the Pacific for nothing, you know."

By now, Mark's hands were shaking so badly that he could barely get his coffee cup to his mouth.

"They say that the *Valencia*'s a phantom ship now, a *Flying Dutchman*, that her image is still seen just off Pachena Point, losing her battle against the sea. I've never seen her myself, but I've heard the tales about her."

"Like what?" Mark asked, his voice coming out much higher-pitched than usual.

"An old-timer around here used to talk about the day he found a cave right at the water's edge. It was low tide, or he wouldn't have noticed it at all. He said if the tide had been any higher, the cave would've been blocked by a boulder. Anyway, this guy claimed that he rowed his dinghy into the cave. Didn't spend too much time inside, though, because the first thing he saw was an old lifeboat floating there, with eight skeletons in it."

The man and his story had even caught Troy's attention by now. "But how's that connected with the *Valencia*?" he asked.

"The name was right there on the bow of the lifeboat: *Valencia*."

Mark leapt to his feet, jostling the table. "I need some air," he said and rushed from the restaurant.

Troy joined him a moment later. "Hey, buddy, what's wrong?"

"Nothing," Mark mumbled.

"Okay. So, how 'bout telling me that ghost story while we're waiting for the bus back to the airport."

"It's in a book I have at home. I'll lend it to you. No, I'll do better than that. I'll give it to you. I don't ever want it back," Mark told his friend emphatically.

"Well, in the meantime, buck up, my fellow camper! We did it. We hiked the West Coast Trail. Definitely the trip of a lifetime, eh?"

"You can say that again."

—

Mark never did tell Troy about the phantom ship or the strange man he had seen on the path, but he would certainly have a story to tell his grandchildren—that is, if his heart ever slowed to its normal beat so he could live long enough to have grandchildren!

EPILOGUE *The Valencia Street Hotel, where the two men had been staying, collapsed in the great San Francisco earthquake in April 1906, four months to the day after the* Valencia *sank. It would seem that those two friends who signed on with that doomed ship were destined to die that year in a structure—either a ship or a building— named* Valencia.

AN ENCOUNTER
WITH THE PAST

Susan was a young woman who was never on time for anything. She was always late for classes, late for dinner, and even late when she and her friends went to a movie.

And so, when it came time for Susan to drive from her home in Lethbridge, Alberta, to her summer job at a sports camp near Penticton, BC, Susan was late in leaving. As a matter of fact, it was nearly nine o'clock in the evening when she finally headed west along Highway No. 3.

Have you ever driven that stretch of highway through the Crowsnest Pass? It's a pretty awe-inspiring route that connects southwestern Alberta and southeastern BC. There's a string of little towns huddled in the mountain valleys, not far from the border between Canada and the US. Many years ago, all those towns were busy coal-mining centres. One was the town of Frank, Alberta, nestled at the foot of Turtle Mountain.

Now, Susan had driven through the Pass many times and she knew the history of the area—that in the middle of the night, more than a century earlier, an avalanche of boulders had come crashing down Turtle Mountain, burying the entire town of Frank and most of its sleeping residents. Even today, piles of enormous boulders remain strewn across the landscape.

That night, as always, a shiver ran down Susan's spine as she drove along the winding road that wove around the awful debris. *What a reminder of Mother Nature's power,* she thought.

Her thoughts were fleeting, though, because as she drove along the curving, hilly Crowsnest Pass highway, Susan suddenly became aware that a really old green truck was following her far too closely for her comfort. A truck that old might not have the best brakes. What if he got too close and hit her? Susan sped up to get away from him. She drove as fast as she dared, up a hill and around a curve, hoping she had shaken the tailgating truck. But she hadn't.

Every time she reached a straight, flat section of road, the truck's lights were there again, shining in her rearview mirror and lighting up the interior of her car. Together, the two vehicles went up, down, and around yet another hilly curve, but the truck was still right behind her. Icicles of fear shot down Susan's spine. The truck was gaining speed steadily. When she looked at the rearview mirror again, all she could see was the monstrous old vehicle's huge grille. She stepped harder on the gas pedal. She had to get away from this maniac!

Then, after she had gone up the next hill and around a curve, she saw that she had finally left him in the distance. She took a deep breath and told herself she was safe. The trucker would never catch her now.

But he did.

This time, when she checked her rearview mirror, he was so

close that she could see the driver. He seemed to be looking over her car, beyond it, as if Susan was not even on the road. Her heart thumped so hard, she could hear it. Someone or something had to end this. Pulling off to the road's narrow shoulders wasn't an option. The truck would hit her car as it barrelled past.

She drove as fast as she dared. The headlights behind her grew dimmer. A few moments later, the truck was gone. Giddy with relief, she slowed the car to a safe speed. To calm herself, she began to sing some of the campfire songs she would teach the campers. Still, though, every once in a while, she checked the road behind her. All was clear. Her shoulders relaxed as she steered easily around another curve in the road. Yes, all was well—until there, just a few feet ahead, she saw people, dozens of people standing near the road. Susan hit the brake pedal and slowed to less than twenty kilometres an hour. The sun had set, but the scene at the side of the road was lit by the dim light of many oil lamps. Men were using horses and rope to move boulders and ancient-looking contraptions to move piles of earth into wagons. Had there been a terrible accident that she hadn't heard about? Was anyone directing traffic through the area?

Susan rolled down her window and kept moving forward at a snail's pace until she came to a flagman. He was close enough to touch her car, and their eyes met for just a moment. Dead silence hung in the air. She could see people working with strange equipment, yet, even with her car window down, she could not hear any sounds at all.

Shivering with fright, she rolled up her window and followed the flagman's directions. She drove slowly until she had passed the bizarre work site. She checked her rearview mirror again.

Nothing was on the road behind her, but she could still clearly see the workers and their odd machines. There was nothing to do now but keep driving away from whatever it was she had just encountered. And so she did. Soon, the weird scene receded into the distance but stayed in her mind as she continued her drive.

Those eerily silent contraptions had just looked wrong. For one thing, they weren't yellow, like the road equipment she was used to seeing. They were green. *Those machines were not of this time.*

And that's when Susan realized that she had somehow driven through a curtain of time. She had witnessed a permanent haunting: spirits from the past forever reliving the aftermath of a traumatic event that must have taken place right after the Turtle Mountain slide had crashed down on Frank back in April 1903.

The terror engendered by that tragedy had scarred the psychic landscape in the area to such a degree that its imprint had become embedded in the very atmosphere of the place, to be replayed over and over again into eternity.

PHANTOM LIFESAVER

Dave clapped his hands twice and called out to his friends, who had scattered along the length of the beach. "Okay, all you happy campers, come and gather around the firepit! I've got some marshmallows and graham crackers for us. It's time to get ready for the best ghost story you've ever heard. Actually, it's the best ghost story *I've* ever heard. In fact, it's no story. It's true, and if it weren't for the ghost I'm going to tell you about, I would never have been born!"

Dave had definitely caught everyone's attention, and in record time, the usually unwieldy crowd of friends was seated around the campfire. Everyone knew Dave was a dramatic storyteller, and they always looked forward to his yarns.

"This story begins years ago, in the winter of 1966, long before any of us were born, I'm sure. Certainly, way before I was born.

"My grandparents, who were not my grandparents at that time but just a young couple in their early twenties, were driving up to Prince Albert, Saskatchewan. They'd heard that there were jobs up there, and a job was something my grandfather, Bill, needed very badly. They already had one child, a son named Scott, and my grandmother, Gwen, was pregnant with my mother. Grandpa had been laid off and, as fond as they were of one another, he and Grandma knew that they couldn't live on love. They packed up their car and drove off in search of a paycheque.

"Like I said, this was the winter of 1966, but the car they were driving was a 1953. A thirteen-year-old car can be reliable transportation these days, but not back then. It was all they had, though. On the day they left, by the time they'd said their good-byes to all their friends and neighbours, it was late afternoon and the winter sky was dark.

"Scott, who would grow up to become my uncle, curled himself around his favourite teddy bear in the back seat. My grandmother softly sang him a lullaby. Soon he was fast asleep. My grandmother made herself comfortable in the passenger's seat beside Grandpa, and the kilometres rolled by in silence. The same worries were on each of my grandparents' minds. Would he be able to find work? And what about accommodation? Who would look after their son when this second child was ready to be born? She would need some help right after the birth. Grandpa's fingers clenched the cold, hard steering wheel while Grandma stared into the bleak landscape ahead.

"The night was inky black and starless," Dave continued. "It had started to snow. The road was narrow, winding, and becoming snow-covered. Inside the car, the little boy slept peacefully. He had no way of knowing how unfounded his sense of security was.

"My grandmother's voice sounded tired as she asked my grandfather, 'Will you be okay driving if I snooze for a bit? I can't stay awake.'

"Grandpa nodded, not daring to look away from the road to meet her loving gaze. The snow was falling heavily now. Breaking his concentration by looking away from the road might have been fatal. They hadn't seen another vehicle for ages.

"He was relieved that his wife had fallen asleep. It gave him a feeling of privacy, and he very much wanted to be alone in his increasing nervousness. He raked himself over the coals, blaming himself for their precarious situation. *How had he managed to put his family in jeopardy like this? What foolishness had possessed him to think that he should try to make the drive in this car, especially in the winter? Why hadn't he left his wife and child behind until he'd found work? What right did he have to be risking their lives this way?*

"As his pregnant wife and toddler son slept, my grandfather drove on. Fear chilled him to the core. Driving was becoming a test for both his skills and his emotional control. When the frightened young man steered around the next curve in the road, he was surprised to see lights at the side of the road. It was a service station! Relief poured over him. He pulled onto the lot slowly and gently enough that neither of his sleeping passengers wakened. Quickly and as quietly as he could, my grandfather stepped out of the car.

"What brings you way out here in this terrible weather?" the service station attendant asked as the two men approached one another.

"The man's innocent and probably well-meaning question was all it took to put my grandfather on the defensive and squelch his plans to ask for help. 'Just fill 'er up,' he replied curtly. He had to raise his voice to be heard against the gusts of wind cutting through them.

"Setting the nozzle into the opening of the old car's gas tank, the station attendant tugged at the fur-lined hood of his heavy jacket until it almost covered his face. 'There's a motel about half a mile up the road,' the man said. 'You'd be wise to stop and spend the night there. A trucker who came through here an hour ago said the weather was even worse farther up the highway— *a raging blizzard* was how he put it. He figured he was just managing to outrun it, but you'll be heading right into it.'

"Perhaps it was because of the cockiness of youth, but the man's sensible suggestion put Grandpa even more on the defensive. No one was going to tell him what was best for his family. He was an adult, a man with a wife, a son, and another baby on the way. He didn't need anyone's advice. He'd make any decisions that had to be made. Besides, the money they'd have to spend on a room for the night would have to come out of an awfully small bundle of cash. They might need that money for food next week, once they were safe and sound and settling into their new home.

"My grandfather managed to at least be polite and thank the man, who merely shrugged in response. Getting back into the car, Grandpa was pleased to see that his wife and son were still asleep. As he turned the key in the ignition and steered back out toward the highway, he glanced in the rearview mirror. The snow was coming down so heavily that within seconds, he'd lost sight of the man who had pumped the gas for him, but he knew by the sudden darkness behind him that he had turned out the lights on his property.

"*Must be headed for the house I saw behind the station,* my grandfather thought as he shifted the car into second gear and pressed gently on the gas pedal. Less than five minutes later, he had passed the soft glow of a neon sign at the side of the road—no doubt the motel that the gas station operator had spoken of.

"The snowfall thickened as he headed along the highway. That nameless trucker that the gas station attendant mentioned was right on the money when he described the storm as a blizzard. Worse, judging from the pinging sound hitting the windshield, it was not just snow that was coming down but ice pellets too. Visibility was virtually zero by now. He was all but driving blind.

"In an attempt to see the road ahead, my grandfather adjusted his headlight switch to high beam, but it only made things worse. The brighter light increased the reflection from the blowing snow, reducing the visibility even more. In desperation, he tried the opposite: he turned his headlights off. That helped! Bill rejoiced inwardly, but only for a second before realizing that although he might be able to see a bit farther ahead on the road, no one could see him. Still, the chances of coming across another vehicle were pretty remote. *No one else would be stupid enough to keep driving through this,* he admitted wryly to himself.

"As his wife and son slept on, the realization that he alone was responsible for the frozen white hell that his stubbornness had created for all of them tormented my grandfather as he drove. The soft sounds of his loved ones' peaceful breathing mocked him. Pebbles of ice beat a staccato rhythm against the car's body and windows.

"On he drove, growing more and more terrified. He'd long since given up hope that just around a bend, any bend, the weather would clear. He knew now that he was driving right into the worst winter storm he'd ever encountered in his short life.

"Over and over he told himself that the only thing he could do was to keep going, so Grandpa just concentrated on keeping his right foot at a steady angle on the gas pedal. Despite this, he was sure they were slowing down, and it was also getting colder and colder in the car. By now it was so cold that his anxious breath was creating clouds in the air in front of his eyes, reducing his limited visibility even more. He pressed harder on the gas, but the car was definitely slowing. Panic rose in his throat. He could hear his own pounding heart. Seconds later, the car came to a dead stop. It had stalled.

"Desperately, he twisted the key in the ignition, but he couldn't get the old engine to turn over, and the grinding of the starter motor wakened his wife and son. 'There's something wrong with the car,' he told Grandma. 'I'm going out to take a look under the hood. You two go back to sleep.'

"He watched as my grandmother blew him a kiss before reaching into the back seat and adjusting the covers around their son. His wife's simple gestures made his feelings of guilt worse.

"Outside, the gale swirled around him as he made his way to the front of the car. Fumbling under the hood, he finally found the release latch and lifted the cover. He stared uncomprehendingly into the engine compartment. Seconds later, a hard gust of biting snow crystals forced him back into the car. He closed the hood as quietly as he could. His wife had moved their son from the back seat and pulled the blankets around them both. Grandpa knew that they would all die if he didn't do something to get them out of the blizzard. *Just a moment longer,* he told himself. *Just let me stay out of that wind a moment longer, and then I'll try again to fix whatever's wrong.*

"Much as he tried not to, Grandpa was beginning to drift into the frozen oblivion of hypothermia when he felt, more than heard, the hood of his car being raised. For a moment, he actually thought that someone was outside his car. But that was impossible. Either he was hallucinating, or dreaming, but stranger still, when he opened his eyes, what he saw seemed to confirm what his other senses had told him. The hood of his car was definitely open.

"Thinking that the wind must have sprung the latch, Grandpa groggily stepped out of the car, intending to close the hood. But, there, leaning over the engine, was a shadowy figure of a man. As my grandfather moved closer, he could hear through the howling wind the sound of a screwdriver working against metal. The form that had been hunched over the front of the car straightened up and spoke. 'Try starting it now,' the blurry presence said.

"Frightened and confused, my grandfather slipped back into the driver's seat and did as he'd been told. The engine coughed twice before firing to life. With tears of relief and joy coursing down his cheeks, he got back out of the car to thank the skilled good Samaritan.

"But the man was gone. Nothing and no one was in front of or beside his now-idling car—no person, no vehicle, not even any tire tracks. Even weirder was the sight of a solitary set of footprints in the snow—made by Grandpa's own boots.

"Bewildered but relieved, he got back into the car, turned it around and drove slowly through the snow in search of the motel he'd passed—a lifetime ago, it felt like. Just minutes later, my grandfather pulled into the parking lot under the neon sign. He said later that he had never seen a more beautiful sight.

"Only when they were snug in their room, with little Scott settled in the middle of the sagging double-bed mattress, did my grandmother thank her brave and much-loved husband for managing to fix the car and get them all to safety. My grandfather accepted the praise without argument. It wasn't that he wanted his wife to believe a lie, but that he knew that the truth would only upset her that night.

"They made Prince Albert by noon the next day. On a spring day a few months later, when they were happily established in their new community, my grandfather finally told my grandmother about his lifesaving encounter with the supernatural. As it turned out, the truth brought my grandparents even closer to one another.

"Their second child, a daughter who would grow up to become my mother, was born a few weeks later. She and my father were still in their teens when they met and fell in love. I was just a little kid when Grandpa told me the story of the blizzard that night back in 1966. After that, whenever I visited them in the winter, if the snow and wind were blowing and howling outside, I'd ask Grandpa and Grandma to tell me the tale of that dark night, because no one in my family would exist today if it hadn't been for that very special good Samaritan—the phantom mechanic."

When Dave had finished telling his family's legend, he looked around at his friends. No one around the firepit spoke or even moved for several minutes.

Finally, a young boy sitting on a lawn chair called out. "So, Uncle Dave, does that mean that I wouldn't have been born either?"

Dave nodded. "That's right, Scott, because your grandfather was the little boy asleep in that car all those years ago."

"They cheated death," a voice in the crowd suggested.

"They really did," someone agreed.

Dave stood up to stretch his legs before adding, "They did indeed. They cheated death, thanks to supernatural assistance."

THE LUMBER KING

We're often warned that it's wise to learn from history. Certainly, there are lessons to be learned from this gruesome incident that took place in a town near a beautiful campground in northern British Columbia.

It seems that many years ago, one of the wealthiest men in town died unexpectedly. He had run the local lumber mill and was so successful that people called him the Lumber King. His death was a terrible shock to the community, and everyone was determined to give him the most dignified and respectful funeral they could.

Toward that end, when the Lumber King's son brought his father's body to the undertaker, he also brought a supply of fine lumber.

"My father was the Lumber King, and I want his coffin to be made from these beautiful pieces of wood," the son instructed. "You are to use all of them to build the King's casket."

The trouble was, the undertaker was not an altogether honest man and, when he saw the extraordinary pieces of lumber, he thought it would be a shame to waste them all on a casket that would be buried underground and eventually rot away—especially when he'd been wanting to build a nice shelf for his woodworking tools.

Once the bereaved son had left and the undertaker was alone with the body, he carefully inspected each piece of wood. Then he selected the finest piece, the one that would make the best shelf. He set that one aside before starting to build the coffin. The sooner he could get the Lumber King's body out of his shop, the better. Even though he was well used to working with the dearly departed, this particular corpse was making him feel decidedly uncomfortable.

When the undertaker went to bed that night, he had trouble falling asleep, and when he finally did, he slept badly. Nightmares of the corpse shouting accusations of thievery at him tormented his unconscious mind while a snowstorm ravaged the outside world. The wind's fury dashed sheets of snow and ice pellets against his windowpanes. In his dreams, undulating silhouettes whispered messages to him but, try as he might, he couldn't quite make out what the dark shapes were saying.

The undertaker woke up suddenly in a cold sweat, sure that it had been the Lumber King's spirit that had disturbed him. He jumped from his bed and lit the lamp that stood on a nearby table. The light flickered three times before dying out completely, and no matter how hard he tried, the undertaker could not get the lamp's wick relit. Soon, he gave up trying and hurried back to his warm bed. An unbearable chill had permeated the room.

When he woke up the next morning, the undertaker was surprised that he felt well—not even a bit tired. He took advantage of his unexpected energy and finished the last bit of work he had left to do. Then he laid the body in the coffin he'd crafted from almost all the wood he'd been given for the job and stood back to admire his handiwork.

He was pleased. No one would ever guess that the coffin was missing one piece of lumber—the best piece.

The snowstorm that had blown in during the night continued to swirl mercilessly through the town. The undertaker knew that even though he desperately wanted to get the body out of his shop, it would be foolish to try to make the delivery while the storm raged. Instead, he decided to spend his time hanging the new shelf he had been wanting. That would keep him distracted until the storm eased enough that he could travel.

As the undertaker worked away, the sounds his tools made seemed to be eerily whispering to him.

"Foolish man," the chisel hissed. "You'll live to regret your theft."

"Die," the vice groaned as the man tightened its clamp.

An eerie, mirthless cackle echoed throughout the dingy room.

He spun around to see where the voices were coming from. Panic overtook him, and he could no longer even think of waiting until the storm had subsided before getting the bedevilled corpse out of his quarters. Desperate to deliver the body, he loaded the coffin onto the wagon that served as his hearse, hitched up his old nag to her harness, and started down the deserted, snow-covered, and wind-whipped road.

The next morning, the milkman found the undertaker's overturned wagon. The horse had broken free of its reins and run off, perhaps in terror, because its master's body lay dead beneath the remnants of the coffin. Beside him lay the Lumber King's body, a sardonic smile frozen on its ice-cold lips.

AMELIA'S MARKER

There's probably not a person on this earth who doesn't have some sort of a reaction when he or she walks through a graveyard. Some people might worry about disturbing the souls of those buried beneath the soil, while others might be forced to contemplate their own mortality. Whatever thoughts or fears we may have, when we're near those who have been laid to rest, graveyards themselves are pretty peaceful places.

Of course, not all bodies are laid to rest so formally. The pioneers of Western Canada often had to make do with less official graves, and farmyard burials were often a necessity. Even so, the mourners would try to mark the plots respectfully with a dignified marker commemorating their loved one.

There's one plot on a tract of land not far from a campground just outside Prince George, BC, that is guaranteed to give anyone a scare they will never forget.

A couple named Amelia and Ernie owned that land way back in the early days of the last century. Amelia was said to have been the kindest and most honest woman who ever walked the earth. Ernie, however, was nothing short of a miserable cuss.

People who knew them both wondered how she could put up with him. Perhaps it was simply that, given the time and place, she had no choice.

One lovely morning in the summer of 1912, a neighbour went to call on Amelia. The door to the farmhouse stood open, so when no one answered her knock, the neighbour went in. There on the kitchen floor lay Amelia's lifeless body. She had been strangled. Ernie was nowhere to be found.

The people from the nearby farms were devastated by the news of Amelia's death. There hadn't been a murder in those parts for as long as anyone could recall. They formed a posse and searched for Ernie, but he was long gone. So they did the only thing they could do. They held a small funeral service for Amelia and buried her remains in the ground just outside her home. Then the local carpenter carved Amelia's name on a makeshift wooden monument and carefully placed the marker at the head of the grave.

A few weeks later, a handful of neighbours met at Amelia and Ernie's old house. They planned to spruce the place up a bit in the hopes that another couple might move to the area and take over the farm. It was a good, solid house, and the land was fertile.

But as it turned out, no one ever lived on that land again, because a strange phenomenon had begun to appear on Amelia's grave marker. At first, there only seemed to be something odd about the grain in the wood, but that oddity evolved until there was an outline of a face forming just above Amelia's name. Over time, that outline became very clear: Ernie's face was readily recognizable. It was as if Amelia was telling everyone, in the only way she could, who had murdered her.

No one ever saw Ernie again. He had gotten away with murder—sort of. The strange grave marker will likely have disintegrated decades ago by now, but still, you might want to silently pay your respects to dear Amelia because it would seem that even in death, she was an honest woman.

DESTINY

There was no doubt about it: Grandma Beth was the most popular person in the family. Everyone always wanted her to be with them, and it was no wonder. She always seemed to know exactly what people needed or wanted, sometimes even before they knew it themselves.

Once, Grandma pulled a box of cutlery out of the enormous purse she always carried. Those knives, forks, and spoons appeared just in time to help feed the people who had gathered for an impromptu get-together. Another time, she had a bottle of baby aspirin in her purse when she visited a young family. By coincidence, when the couple's son awoke from his nap, he was feverish; the aspirin was just the thing to bring down his temperature. Beth's granddaughters always knew that they could count on their grandma to have a ponytail elastic for any little girl who needed her hair out of the way, whether it was for a gymnastics routine or to play softball. The list of Grandma's small favours over the years was practically endless. When anyone questioned her about her special ability to predict exactly what her loved ones would need, she would just smile and say, "I guess I'm just a bit more sensitive than most people."

Most months of the year, Grandma Beth drove up and down the highway between Regina and Saskatoon whenever a member of her family needed her. She used to say that her little yellow Volkswagen Beetle convertible knew the route on its own. When summer arrived, Grandma Beth, or Gran, as the kids sometimes called her, stationed herself at a campsite in Candle Lake Provincial Park, in Saskatchewan, and waited for her family to spread themselves around her—and spread they did. She would stay a few days with each of her sons and daughters until all her grandchildren felt sure that they were the one that Gran loved most.

During those summers at the lake, Grandma Beth had just two rules: she had to have a good strong cup of coffee as soon as she woke up in the morning, and she needed her morning swim. After that, she was ready to play all day.

On the Canada Day long weekend a few years ago, the fun at the lake had just begun. Grandma was starting out the summer by staying with Mark and Shirley in their RV. After she'd gulped down her coffee, Beth headed for the lake, towels in hand.

The cold water always felt refreshing, and the exercise invigorated her for the day. She stood on the beach drying herself off when a flicker of movement nearby caught her eye. She looked around. There was a little girl standing not more than three metres from her.

"Oh, hello," she said to the child. "I didn't see you there before."

The girl just stood silently, with her hands on her hips, and stared at the older woman as though there was something very puzzling about Grandma Beth.

"I'm Beth," she tried again. "You must be staying at the lake with your parents." *Strange little mite*, she thought. *All skin and bones, that one. Why, she's so thin you can all but see through her.*

The child continued to stare. Beth shifted from one foot to another. Suddenly feeling uncomfortably exposed, Beth wrapped her towel tightly around herself, but the little girl just held her gaze. *The child's eyes are odd, almost a shade of gold. And piercing. Such a strange expression on her face. She looks perplexed. Maybe the direct approach is best*, Beth thought.

"What's your name?"

This time the child responded, but so quietly that Beth could hardly hear her. *Did she say her name's Destiny?*

"Why, that's a pretty name."

"It's not one you're likely to forget." Again, the girl's voice was barely audible, as if she were talking to herself, not Beth.

Beth's mind was racing. *It's not often that a child makes me feel uneasy, but this one certainly does, and what's even more unusual is that I can't predict for the life of me what she might need.* She bent down to pick up her other towel. When she stood up, the girl was gone. The beach was empty. Destiny was simply nowhere to be seen. Beth's stomach clenched. That couldn't be. She looked along the beach and up toward the campsites. A person could not disappear that quickly!

A moment later, Grandma Beth's well-honed sensitivity kicked in: she realized that Destiny was not a real child. She wasn't a person at all. She was a manifestation. She was destiny. She was Beth's destiny.

Terrified, Beth ran from the beach as quickly as her elderly legs would carry her.

"Mark! Shirley! Come quick. I have to leave—right now."

"For goodness' sake, what's wrong?" Shirley asked, giving Beth a hug.

Mark looked up from the book he'd been reading and said, "Mom, you just need that second mug of brew."

"No, no, I don't," Grandma insisted. "I have to get away from here right now. I have to go to the other side of the lake, to Dana and Paul's place."

"What's happened?" By now, Mark realized that something was seriously wrong. Certainly, nothing as simple as a cup of coffee was going to solve this problem.

Fighting back hysterics, Beth told her son, "I'm frightened. Take me to the other side of the lake. Take me to Dana's. Now! Please!"

Mark turned to his wife. "Shirley, you drive Mom around to Dana's. I want to check out the beach and see what this is all about."

Shirley nodded and held out her hand to her mother-in-law. "Come on, Beth. No more need to fret. We'll be over at Dana's in a minute. We're just sorry you're leaving so soon."

Mark hurried down to the beach. It was deserted except for a small child, a little girl.

"Hello," he called toward her.

The child didn't return his greeting. Nor did she move from where she stood, her hands placed firmly on her hips.

"Who are you? You were very rude to my mother. You scared her half to death."

The child's eyes glimmered like gold in the morning sun.

"I didn't mean to scare her. She surprised me is all."

"Who are you?" Mark repeated.

"I'm Destiny," the child said. "I was surprised to see your mother here this morning, because I have an appointment with her later this afternoon, across the lake at your sister's campsite."

"What?" was all Mark could mutter as he hurriedly backed away from the beach.

Over at Dana's campsite, Shirley did her best to make Grandma Beth comfortable. Dana shook her head and said, "That just doesn't sound like Mom, panicking like that."

"I know. Mark and I thought the same thing, but she was insistent that she wanted to come here," Shirley confided.

"Of course. She's welcome here anytime. I'll just keep an eye on her and see that she doesn't overextend herself," Dana said as she patted her mother's shoulder. "We'll be fine, I'm sure."

Beth sat in a deck chair for most of the afternoon, not saying a word to anyone. Then Dana thought she heard her mother mumble, "You again?"

Moments later, Grandma Beth sat bolt upright. Her face was as pale as death. Her hands shook as she reached for her enormous purse, hefted it onto her lap, and pulled out a loonie. "Quick," she said, handing the coin to Dana. "Fetch one of the kids to go to the store. I need to get a lottery ticket."

Dana jumped to her feet. Something was clearly very wrong. Should she call an ambulance? Would it get here fast enough? "Mother, what is wrong with you today?"

"There's no time for questions," Grandma Beth said firmly. "I'll be fine. Send one of the kids to buy me a lottery ticket."

"If you want a lottery ticket so badly, why don't you and I walk to the store together," Dana suggested. "I'll buy you five lottery tickets if you want them."

"No. I have to use this loonie, and one of the little ones must get it for me."

Dana sighed and called her ten-year-old son, Brent, to her side. "Grandma Beth wants you to run to the store for her. Just buy her a one-dollar lottery ticket and come right back, you hear?"

Brent nodded. Clutching the coin, he trotted as fast as he could down the country road toward the general store. Half an hour later, he was back.

"Here, Grandma," he said, dropping the slightly creased scratch-and-win ticket onto Beth's lap.

She looked at it for a long time before picking it up and holding it to her chest. "This is my destiny," she said. "Brent, scratch that ticket for me, will you?"

The little boy scratched away at the card with the side of his thumbnail and then stared at it. "I don't get these games," he said. He handed the scratched ticket to his mother. She looked at it, rubbed her eyes, and looked again before collapsing into the chair beside Grandma Beth.

"You've won!" she exclaimed, showing the ticket to the older woman.

"I knew I shouldn't fear Destiny," Grandma Beth said with a smile.

THE VAMPIRE

Gus and Marie, along with Marie's older sister, Teresa, and her husband, Juan, had hiked to the backwoods just west of the town of Smithers, BC. They were all well-experienced campers, but they'd had a gruelling trek to their campsite. They needed to eat and then get some sleep. But their dinner, cooked over a roaring campfire, was so delicious, it perked them up, so they decided to linger around the fire for a while.

"Whose turn is it to tell a ghost story?" Teresa asked.

Before anyone had time to answer, Gus signalled thumbs down.

"Why does it always have to be a ghost story?" he asked. "What about something about aliens or werewolves? I don't know, just a bit of variety would be nice for a change."

"Oh, Gus, you're just afraid of ghosts," Marie teased.

"I know a good story with not so much as one ghost," Juan offered.

"Is the story true?" Teresa asked.

"Indeed it is. I read it in a book."

"Then you're our storyteller," Gus said. "Although I've got

to warn you, I'm really tired, so if I nod off while you're spinning your yarn, don't be offended."

"This is no yarn, my friend. It's a true story, and trust me, you're not likely to fall asleep."

And so, while the embers in the campfire burned low and the owls hooted through the trees, Gus recounted this tale.

Three adult siblings, Edward, Michael, and Caitlyn, lived in a bungalow on the outskirts of an isolated prairie town. They always locked the windows at night, even though their closest neighbour was an old graveyard surrounded by a stone wall.

One hot summer's night, Caitlyn's room was sweltering. She tossed and turned and simply could not drift off to sleep. The moon was high and full, and it bathed the yard in a lovely silver light. The young woman propped herself up on pillows and stared at the enchanting sight.

Then, in the distance, near a grove of trees, Caitlyn noticed something odd: two pinpoints of yellow light. She watched for several minutes as the twin orbs danced about in the trees. Soon she realized that the yellow dots were getting larger. She blinked and rubbed her eyes. The yellow dots were moving straight toward her window.

She leapt from the bed and ran to her bedroom door, but it was jammed shut. She screamed for her brothers before daring to look back toward the window. Two flaming yellow eyes set in a wizened, brown face pressed up against the glass. She tried the door again, but her hands were shaking too violently to open it. Then she heard scratching at the window glass. She spun around. There, only a metre or two away from her, was a fiendish-looking creature. It was horrifying. It was hideous. Terror consumed her.

Caitlyn could hear her brothers calling to her from the other side of her bedroom door, telling her to open the door, but she couldn't.

Then the scratching stopped.

In its place was an insistent pecking sound. The creature with the yellow eyes was picking at the putty that held the window glass in place. She screamed until she could scream no more, and that's when she heard the window shatter. The thing's claw-like hands pulled its rail-thin body through the opening. It was now in Caitlyn's room.

The young woman fainted and dropped to the floor.

Michael and Edward pounded more ferociously at the door as the sounds of a gruesome attack echoed in their ears. Finally, the door gave way.

The brothers burst into the room and found Caitlyn crumpled on the floor, bleeding profusely. Her face, throat, and shoulders had been viciously slashed and punctured. Edward bent to help her while Michael ran to the window and saw the attacker fleeing into the night.

Michael ran after the creature, but the tall figure took impossibly long strides and was soon lost from sight near the graveyard wall. Frustrated, Michael returned to help his injured sister.

Some weeks later, a local farmer paid a visit to the siblings' home.

"I know you've had trouble," he said to the brothers. "I think it's the same trouble I've had in the past."

Michael and Edward listened to the man's incredible story. The farmer said that there had been an intruder in his own home two years before and that whoever it was had attacked his daughter in the same vicious way that Caitlyn had been attacked.

"She was bitten on her face and neck and shoulders," he explained. "She'll never look right again. And she's never been able to describe the fiend that did it."

What was more, the farmer said, there were other women who had awakened to a terrifying sight, a monster shaped like a man.

"But those women, they screamed out in time," the neighbour explained.

Not knowing what else they could do, Edward and Michael moved their beds into a room directly across the hall from Caitlyn's, and they also kept two loaded pistols by their door.

The winter passed quietly. Then, one chilly April night, Caitlyn was awakened by that same menacing sound of scratching on glass. She screamed instantly. Michael ran to her side, and Edward made for the front door, pistol in hand.

Out on the grounds he saw a tall, thin creature bounding toward the trees. Edward fired his gun. He was sure he had hit his mark. The creature stumbled but regained its balance and carried on, but at a slower pace. Edward gave chase, certain that he could overtake the injured thing.

The creature limped toward the wall that surrounded the graveyard. Edward watched in horror as it crept up the side of the wall and scrambled over the top. Edward raced to the cemetery gates. He got there just in time to see a tall, sinister shadow slip through the doors of a large burial vault.

The next day, Edward and Michael gathered a group of townsfolk together. Each carrying a gun and a lantern, the men made their way to the cemetery, past row upon row of crumbling gravestones.

"Here," Edward said, pointing to the vault.

Two of the strongest men went to work on the doors, prying away thick iron cables until the corroded hinges gave way with a groan.

The brothers stood together at the opening of the tomb, their pistols drawn and ready. Three other men stepped forward to join them. They entered the dank, gloomy vault in single file.

The screaming began within seconds.

The men waiting for them in the cemetery watched in horror as one of their friends emerged from the darkness babbling incoherently, howling and shrieking in terror. He bolted from the graveyard. Then Michael and Edward emerged from the tomb.

"We'll be needing wooden stakes," Edward said, "and wood for a funeral pyre."

The men stared at him in horror.

"Surely not!" said one.

The brothers nodded. Inside the chamber, they had found the wreckage of splintered coffins and the gruesome remnants of corpses scattered about. In the midst of the grotesque sight, one coffin stood untouched. Inside that coffin lay the body of a tall, thin man with a shrivelled, brown face and claw-like hands. His clothing was old-fashioned, but his body was preserved.

The men examined the corpse's peculiarly long, curved teeth, and that's when they noticed a dark liquid streaming from the corners of the man's mouth. It was fresh, red blood.

"A vampire," one man whispered. The brothers nodded.

They brought the body above ground and built a fire. Michael thrust a wooden stake through the vampire's chest. Just before the men threw the impaled, skeletal figure into the flames, Michael noticed a peculiar hole in its ragged trousers.

"Wait," he commanded. He tore the cloth away from the body. Beneath the trouser leg was a hole in the mummified flesh, a gunshot wound. He *had* hit his mark.

Together, the men hurled the creature into the fire. Then they watched as the flames engulfed the unholy beast.

—

Juan let the last syllable of his story reverberate around the campfire. No one spoke. And no one had nodded off.

Then Gus waved his hand in the air as if to clear away the spooky tale. "That's just the story of Dracula," he protested.

"Not on your life," Juan countered. "This is a true story that was well documented decades before Bram Stoker ever put quill to paper."

He paused and then added, "And that's the truth."

UNREAL ESTATE AGENT

Vera loved her job as the estate agent at a group of cabins near a beautiful lake in Southern Saskatchewan. But no matter how dedicated anyone is to the job, getting away from work after a busy week is always welcome. And so it was that Vera hummed a catchy tune as she tidied her paperwork late one Friday afternoon. She always liked to come back to an organized office on Monday mornings. She gave one last look around, found everything satisfactory, and headed toward the door—just as an angry-looking client burst into her office. It was Raoul. *Of course it was Raoul, prissy old Raoul.*

"We need to talk," he insisted. "That cabin you put me in is horrible!"

Vera sighed. If only she'd left five minutes sooner. But she hadn't, and this was clearly a problem that couldn't wait until Monday. She invited the man in.

"Do tell me what's wrong, Raoul," Vera said, trying to sound sympathetic.

"What's *wrong*?" he shrieked. "*Everything* is wrong, and it's all your fault! You know all about what goes on in that cabin!

You *must* know! And yet you let me move in without a word of warning!"

"I assure you that I would never knowingly..."

"Oh, really?" the client interrupted. "You told me that cabin has the best view of any in the campground. I was lucky it was vacant, you said. Hah! If the place was so perfect, then why didn't you take that one yourself?"

"Please try to calm yourself, Raoul. Just start from the beginning and tell me what's happened. I'm sure something can be done."

His fury apparently somewhat spent, Raoul relaxed a bit. "That's the problem," he said as he slumped in the chair. "I don't think there's anything anyone can do. And it's terrible. Truly, I've seen things..." He buried his face in his hands.

Vera quietly moved a box of tissues closer to her distraught client. "From the beginning please, Raoul."

His complexion was pale, and there were deep shadows beneath his eyes.

"I first noticed something wrong about a month ago," he said. "It was only days—certainly no more than a few days—after I moved in. Do you remember that magnificent thunderstorm we had? It knocked the power out."

Vera nodded.

"Well," he continued, "I do so enjoy a lovely storm. And after the lights went out, it was even better. Much more dramatic. So I was happily watching the lightning through the big picture window when..."

"Go on," she urged.

When Raoul began to speak again, his voice was filled with emotion.

"Suddenly, there were lights everywhere!" he said. "Spots of light flared up like candle flames, all over the house. I didn't know what to make of it; it seemed impossible. I was turning this way and that way—every time I saw a new light flash in the periphery of my vision, I would spin around to see what was causing it. My heart was pounding, I can tell you. And then, suddenly, I sensed something behind me. I knew it was a presence. I turned slowly, and there it was. A face."

Raoul shuddered at the recollection.

"What sort of face?" Vera asked after several seconds.

Her client squeezed his eyes shut.

"The most terrible face you can imagine," he said. "So fleshy and florid. Vacuous. It looked right through me with these empty, unseeing eyes, as though I wasn't even there. I can tell you, it's an experience I never want to have again. It chilled me to the bone."

"What happened next?" From a business point of view, Vera didn't want to be there anymore. She was already imagining the property value depreciating, particularly if word of this spread—and it was bound to. But in truth, she loved a scary story as much as anyone did, and her curiosity had been piqued. "Tell me," she urged.

"The electricity came back on," Raoul said. "Then the other lights—the eerie, flickering flames—went out then, one by one. It was really quite disconcerting."

"So that was it, then?" she asked, hoping that if nothing else had happened, her business might be safe after all and Raoul might be convinced to stay. He might think that it had all been a figment of his imagination. Then he interrupted her hopeful reverie.

"How I wish. But that was only the beginning."

Vera pressed her fingers wearily against her temples.

"Then go on," she said.

Raoul shook his head in frustration.

"It's difficult to talk about," he said, wringing his hands. "The noises! The horrible noises that I have had to put up with! Voices, constant voices. And music, the most dreadful music I have ever heard, blaring at all hours of the day and night. The television comes on, too, very unexpectedly and during the most offensive programs."

Raoul's dismay was evident.

"I can assure you that I have tried all sensible solutions," he said, sounding dejected. "But everything I do seems to aggravate the situation, and I get hours of doors slamming and frantic-sounding voices."

Vera spoke slowly and carefully. "Can you understand what they're saying?"

Raoul's posture stiffened.

"Only recently," he said. "They've become clearer—closer, it seems. I can understand a word here and there. I dare say that they are planning to drive me out. Out of my own home—can you believe it? They plan to drive me out!"

Vera looked thoughtfully at her client. "Will you let them drive you out?"

Raoul's hands flew to his chest. "What choice do I have?"

"You could stay," Vera suggested quietly. "You could have some fun with it."

"*Fun?* You don't seem to understand. I'm terrified!"

"They're probably more terrified of you!"

"Why on earth would they fear me?"

Vera laughed in spite of herself.

"Raoul," she said. "You're a GHOST!"

The client looked offended. "I prefer 'ethereal entity,' if you don't mind," he sniffed. "And it doesn't mean that I'm interested in common haunting. That's why I requested a vacant cabin, not one filled with wild, terrifying, unattractive living beings."

"Okay, okay." Vera held up her hands in surrender. "I'll be honest; I was hoping you wouldn't notice them. Not everyone does, you know. And I didn't exactly have a vacancy the day you came."

"I knew it!"

"But I do have a vacancy now, so let me make it up to you—what do you say? Two months of free rent in a new place—to compensate for any inconvenience you may have suffered."

"Inconvenience? Terror is what it was," the client pouted. "I thought I was losing my mind!"

Silence hung in the air between the two. Raoul blinked. The solution made sense. He took a deep breath and waved his hands in a fluttery gesture, as if to shoo away any remaining unpleasantness.

"Fine," he said. "Tell me about this other cabin."

And so she did, in detail. "It's an old, abandoned place with broken windows and no plumbing. I assure you it is utterly uninhabitable by the living."

"That does sound nice." Raoul breathed a sigh of relief. "I could use a restful time after all I've been through."

And so a deal was struck. When the client left the real estate office, both he and the agent felt pleased and relieved.

As Vera watched Raoul float away, she looked at the clock and sighed.

Now she'd be late for the party. The man whose home she haunted was hosting a dinner party for some co-workers. Vera had been planning for weeks to attend. She hoped to cause some random cold spots and perhaps play with the lights a bit. Why, she might even levitate that hateful cat that was always staring at her. Revenge could be so sweet, and it would certainly give the wage slaves something to discuss around the water cooler on Monday. But now, thanks to all the time she'd taken to sort out Raoul's problem, she would have to rush, and she never did her best work when she felt rushed.

But then Vera realized that there was no need to hurry. *I'll let them enjoy their meal, and then I'll float Fluffy around after the coffee is served.* The image made her smile.

You see, unlike some of her clients (not to mention any names, Raoul), she enjoyed haunting. She even had to stop herself from doing it too often.

As for the cabin Raoul had been in, the place with the troublesome, boisterous family, she had just the ghost for that one. A tough, old spectral spinster named Annabelle, who had died so long ago that she had only distant, faded, watercolour memories of her earthly body. In fact, Annabelle had once told Vera that she didn't even believe in the living. Yes, Annabelle would make the perfect replacement.

Vera smiled to herself again and resumed humming her catchy tune as she turned out the office lights and flipped the sign in the window to read CLOSED.

The best way to end the week, she thought as she drifted out the door, *is with all the problems solved.*

FRECKLES

Anyone who has ever owned a pet knows that it doesn't take long for the little critters to become important family members, and this was certainly true of the Duncan family. Ben and Grace had adopted Freckles, a collie, shortly after their wedding. The puppy was no more than a little ball of fur the day they brought him home, but he soon grew into a handsome and exceptionally loyal dog.

A year later, when the couple was expecting their first child, they were concerned that Freckles might be jealous of the baby, but when Natalie was born, the dog took to her right away. Over the next few years, the Duncans welcomed two more children to their family, William and Sarah. Freckles was equally fond of the younger two and very protective of the entire family. The only time the dog ever barked or growled was when a stranger came into the yard or near any of the children.

Sadly, early in the summer when Natalie turned thirteen and William and Sarah were both less than ten, Freckles died. Everyone in the family was devastated. Ben and Grace both took time off from their jobs to be with the three children, but for weeks on end, the entire household was sad. No matter where they went in the house or the yard, they pictured Freckles there and knew he never would be again. Finally, Grace decided that the family needed a vacation, and, as the whole family loved the outdoors, she decided they should go camping in Wood Buffalo National Park, at the border between northern Alberta and the Northwest Territories.

As soon as the family set up camp by beautiful Pine Lake, Ben and Grace knew they'd done the right thing. The children were running through the woods, swimming in the lake, happy and laughing in a way they hadn't since Freckles died. They went on lots of long hikes together, so everyone was tuckered out at the end of the day and slept better than ever before.

One morning, Natalie woke up early. She shook her brother and sister awake and suggested that they let their parents sleep while they went for a hike of their own. They set off into the forest without so much as a bottle of water or any insect repellant. Soon, Sarah, the youngest child, was getting hungry and thirsty, and the mosquitoes biting at her arms and legs were making her cranky. Natalie decided they'd better make their way back to the campsite. The trio turned around, but after walking for some time, they realized that they weren't on the route to their campsite. They retraced their steps and tried again, but still nothing looked familiar.

Soon Sarah and William were both crying, and Natalie was frantic. She knew she was responsible. Not only had the hike been her idea, but she was the oldest and should have known better. Trying to act more confident than she felt, she looked around, hoping to find the right path. But it was hopeless. They were completely lost. Fighting back panic, Natalie remembered what her parents had told her to do in case she ever did get lost.

"Stay in one place," they had cautioned. "That will make it easier to find you."

So that is what the three children did. They sat huddled together, crouching at the base of a gigantic coniferous tree.

When Ben and Grace woke up and saw that the children's sleeping bags were empty, they couldn't believe their eyes. At first, they weren't sure whether the kids might be just playing a joke on them, so they waited for a few minutes; but soon, Grace became anxious and began calling their names. When no one answered her, Ben called their names as loudly as he could and then added, "If you think this is funny, it's not. Your mother and I are worried about you."

When there still wasn't any answer, Grace and Ben knew there was a serious problem. Ben got in the car and drove to get help while Grace stayed behind at the campsite in case the children came back.

Before long, a group of experienced searchers began combing through the forest. They searched in an organized pattern to cover the area efficiently—all but one, that is.

A man named Jake walked in a slightly different direction from the rest of the group. He would walk a few paces and then stand still, listening in case the missing children were calling. He couldn't hear any voices, but he did hear a jingling sound, like a tiny bell ringing.

Then a movement in a nearby bush caught his eye. It was a dog, a collie. Jake called the dog to come. It had a collar on with two tags attached to it. *Those must've made the jingling sounds he had heard*, he thought. He bent down and read the tags. One was the dog's licence, and the other had the dog's name on it: Freckles.

Jake presumed the collie was lost, so he tried to get Freckles to follow him, but the dog wouldn't stay by his side. Instead, the animal would run about thirty metres from him and then bark. When Jake stood still, Freckles would run back to him and then away again and bark once more.

That dog wants me to follow it, Jake thought, and so he did. Freckles ran ahead, but not so far ahead that Jake couldn't see him. The unlikely pair was well into the dense forest when Freckles ran around an enormous coniferous tree—and disappeared. Jake hurried to where he'd last seen the dog, but Freckles had simply vanished.

He walked around the base of the tree and there, huddled together at the far side of the trunk, were Natalie, William, and Sarah. All three children were frightened, thirsty, and covered with mosquito bites but otherwise unharmed. Jake scooped them up in a bear hug, and together they called to the other searchers.

When everyone was back at their campsite, the relieved parents thanked the searchers warmly. They asked Jake how he knew where to find the children.

Jake shook his head in confusion. "It was the strangest thing. I saw a dog in the forest. He must've been someone's pet, because he had a collar and dog tags. I can't imagine what he was doing so far away from town, but I'm grateful he was there because that dog led me right to the children."

"A dog?" Ben asked. "Someone's pet, you say?"

"Yes, definitely someone's pet. He was a beautiful dog, a collie. I can't imagine where he is now. He went around that big tree and then just plain vanished. I hope he's not lost. The name on his tag was Freckles."

The searchers gave Jake a quizzical look, but Ben and Grace understood exactly what had happened.

Even in death, Freckles was determined to protect the family he loved.

WAMPOHAMA

Rick finished hammering down the tent pegs and joined Katerina at the picnic bench, where she'd been sitting with her nose in the book she had found at a used bookstore in town.

"What's the book called?" he asked absently. She angled the book for him to see.

"*A Short Account of the Old Indian Witch, Wampo . . . Wampo* . . . What? Is the book as long as the title?"

"Not quite," Katerina answered, with some annoyance in her voice. "And the witch's name was Wampohama."

She didn't see any point in offering more information. Rick hadn't been interested in anything she had said for ages. In reality, their relationship had all but expired. Katerina even suspected that Rick had a new girlfriend. If this camping trip hadn't been planned since January, she would have already told him to take a hike.

"What the heck are you reading about witches for, anyway?" he asked.

Katerina looked at him, trying to determine whether his curiosity was in the least bit genuine. After a moment's assessment, she decided to give him a real answer.

"It's history," she explained. "Wampohama was an old Indigenous woman who died more than three hundred years ago. What makes her story especially interesting is that she lived right where Winnipeg stands today. The white settlers called her Mother Damnable. She made all sorts of predictions, so she was a prophet."

"Right," Rick said sarcastically.

What did I expect? Katerina asked herself. She knew that Rick was not known for his open mind. At least she had learned not to argue with him. Instead, she responded calmly.

"Come on, Rick. Don't you think it's possible to know things through—I don't know—a sixth sense? Don't you believe even a little bit in intuition?"

"I believe half of what I see," he sneered, "and none of what I hear." Looking satisfied at having made his point, Rick walked away.

A familiar slow, angry burn simmered in the pit of Katerina's stomach, but it was not just due to Rick's quick dismissal of her ideas. *I know something about you,* she thought. *I haven't seen it, I haven't heard it, and I can't prove a thing. Yet. But I know.* She returned to her reading.

An hour later, as Katerina unrolled the sleeping bags, Rick poked his head into the tent. "There's a game of shinny at the arena in town. I'm going to join the guys."

"Hockey in August?" Katerina asked. Once again, she managed to keep her voice calm.

"Why not? You know me, if there's a game going, I want to be in it. I'll be late, so don't wait up." Rick walked toward his truck without a backward glance.

He was lying. For the first time, Katerina knew that as a fact. On their way through town, they had passed the arena. There had been a sign on it reading CLOSED FOR MAINTENANCE TILL SEPTEMBER.

If only she could figure out who his new girlfriend was. If she confronted Rick without knowing the woman's name, he would deny everything and cover his tracks, and right now all she had was a hunch, a suspicion.

Katerina held her book as she stood by the tent, watching Rick's truck disappear in the distance. Then she tucked into her sleeping bag, lit the lantern, and continued to read.

Her book, the one with the impossible title, *A Short Account of the Old Indian Witch, Wampohama: Better Known to the Early Settlers as Mother Damnable, Together with her Extraordinary Prophecies, Already Partially Fulfilled, Concerning the Future Destinies of What are Now Winnipeg, Manitoba, and the Great North-West,* didn't have very many pages in it, but the information was fascinating. And, it gave her an idea.

Katerina took her lantern and went outside into the dark night. She found twelve smooth stones and laid them in a circle on the picnic bench. Then she thought of Mother Damnable and opened her mind to the long-dead witch. It wasn't long before she could feel a new energy in the air.

She closed her eyes and quietly began to chant, "Wampohama, Wampohama . . . Mother Damnable. You know everything, and I need to know one more thing." Two of the stones on the table rocked back and forth. Katerina's body swayed slowly and rhythmically.

A misty cloud formed in the lantern's light. Then an image began to appear in the mist. Soon she could make out an old woman's deeply lined face. At first the image wavered, nearly liquid at its outer edges, but with each passing minute, it became sharper, stronger, and more powerful.

"Mavis," the image said and laughed with a mirthless cackle before disappearing back into the mist.

Katerina smiled. Then she laughed out loud, not noticing that her laugh had an unfamiliar cackle to it. She would bide her time, but if Rick ever criticized her choice of reading material, she'd have a very interesting story to tell him, and the name Mavis would be that story's punchline.

THE  HITCHHIKER

Alexander had grown up in a tiny town nestled in central British Columbia. The place was a company town, but it had everything a person could need: stores, a service station, a doctor's office, even a cemetery. Alex could have done without that creepy cemetery, but all in all, he enjoyed living there and never saw any reason to move away.

One dark, moonless night, Alexander was walking along a dirt road near town. He wasn't sure how long he had been walking. It seemed like forever, but he knew it was probably only an hour or so. His car—what was left of it, anyway—was no more than a couple of kilometres back, but with no moon to guide him and a couple of broken ribs making him wince with every step, the progress had been slow and painful. The rain made it worse. It was coming down, not in drops, but in sheets, drenching Alexander's light clothing and plastering his hair to his throbbing skull. The rutted dirt road was covered in slippery muck that was persistently working its way into his shoes. With every step, he felt worms of mud squish up between his toes.

He was shivering from the cold and wet, miserable with pain, and desperate to get to a telephone. Now, on top of all that, he had come to that creepy cemetery. Alex accepted the inevitability of death, but not the burial part. The idea of taking a permanent nap underground absolutely terrified him. He always preferred to avoid the place, but now he had no option.

Alex wiped the rainwater from his eyes and took a deep breath, flinching with pain as his lungs pushed against his ribcage. He paused. There was really no decision to make: he knew that he needed to get back to town. He needed to see the doctor to have his ribs taped up. But first, he needed to walk past the graveyard. "Just do it. Just walk," he told himself. And eventually, he did. He put one muddy foot in front of the other and slowly began to make his way forward. He kept his eyes trained straight ahead, ignoring the overgrown tombstones and sculptures that loomed in the darkness. *He could do it. No problem.*

And there was no problem—until a sudden, blinding light flashed behind him. Alex shrieked, but his voice was swallowed by a low rumbling noise that grew louder with each second. There was something familiar about the sound emerging from the rain. It was a motor. In one single, gratitude-filled moment, he realized there was a car coming up the road behind him. He felt weak with relief. He wanted to sink to his knees and weep with joy, but he couldn't waste that kind of time or energy. Instead, he turned to face the vehicle and moved to stand directly in the blinding wash of its headlights. Painfully, he raised his arms above his head and waved them back and forth. He thought this gesture would be better than sticking out his thumb. He wanted to make it clear that he was no common hitchhiker.

The car slowed as it approached. Alexander held up one hand to block the glare of the headlights and squinted in the direction of the darkened windshield, trying to see the driver. As his eyes began to adjust, the car came to a full stop. Alex stepped over to the passenger-side door, crouched as much as his painful ribs would allow, and peered into the vehicle. There was a mechanical buzz as the window magically rolled halfway down to reveal a pale-faced young man with a worried expression looking out at him.

The driver nodded, but his brow was knit in a way that indicated he hadn't quite decided whether to stay stopped or not. "Car trouble?" he asked, as he looked Alexander over.

Alex wiped his dripping hair away from his face and nodded. "Yeah, you could say that," he said. "My car's back there, halfway down a hill and wrapped around a tree. It's been quite a night. If you could just give me a ride to town . . . " His voice trailed off. He was too exhausted to explain further. He stood, soaking wet, as the stranger sized him up and made a decision.

"You look too messed up to be dangerous," the driver finally said. "Get in. Grab a blanket out of the back and wrap yourself up."

Alexander reached behind the passenger seat and pulled out an old Hudson's Bay blanket. He wrapped it around himself, grateful for the warmth, though he was fully aware that the driver was more concerned about his car's upholstery than Alexander's comfort. As he settled into the low-slung passenger seat, he could understand why. The car had to be some kind of custom job. Alexander had never been in a vehicle with such sleek lines and strange gadgets. European, he supposed. Even the pulsing music on the radio was oddly foreign.

"So you went off the road, huh?" said the kid as he put the car back in gear and began to drive. "Your ride must be way down the ravine; I didn't see a thing back there."

He cast a sideways glance at Alexander and shook his head. "You look busted up, man."

Alexander watched out the window and let his breath out in a silent whoosh once they had cleared the cemetery. "Sorry— what?" he asked, suddenly aware of the silent space that meant it was his turn to talk.

"Are you, like, hurt bad?" the kid asked.

Alexander nodded. The simple motion made a bright pain flare behind his eyes. His head began to throb in sync with the strange music. "Yeah, I think I hit my head. Maybe cracked a couple of ribs."

The kid shook his head sympathetically. "You're lucky I came along," he said. "My family has a cabin nearby. That's the only reason I'm on this old dirt road. I've never seen anyone else out here. I didn't think people used this route anymore. Where were you headed, anyway? Did you get lost or something? Take a wrong turn?"

"No, I wasn't lost," Alexander said. "I was heading up to . . . "

The kid waited patiently for Alexander to finish the sentence. But he couldn't. He brought his hands up to his face and massaged his temples with his fingers, but it didn't help. He couldn't remember where he had been going. And there was something in the way the young man was looking at him, something about the sheen of his pale face in the eerie reflection of dashboard lights that made Alexander feel blank and lost. He shook himself, trying to lose the feeling. "Sorry," he said. "Bump on the head, you know. My memory isn't working the way it should."

"Don't sweat it," the kid said. He spoke lightly, but there was something in his voice that made Alexander shiver.

The cemetery, Alexander thought. *I met him right beside the cemetery. That's just a coincidence, the kid couldn't possibly be a ghost. It's a ridiculous thought. He's driving a car.* Alex scolded himself immediately for his foolishness. When he emerged from his paranoid thoughts, the young man was talking again.

"You said you're going home?" he asked.

"Yes!" Alexander nodded with relief.

The kid shook his head. "But there's no town near here anymore. There used to be, but that was ages ago. It's barely even a ghost town by now."

Alexander was confused. "That's my hometown. There's a service station right by the tracks, after you turn off the highway. And a diner that stays open late—it's got pay phones. There's even a doctor who lives nearby."

The kid was looking at Alexander strangely, shaking his head. Something shiny bobbed alongside his jaw as he spoke. Alexander noted with amazement that the kid had his ear pierced just like a woman's.

"Nah, man," he said. "I'm telling you, it's gone."

Why would the kid make up a story like that? There was something wrong with him. Suddenly, Alexander didn't want to be in the car with him anymore. He wanted to be back out in the rain, wet, and cold, feeling the mud squirm between his toes. He wanted to be walking, holding his arms tightly against his aching ribs, sloshing one tired foot in front of the other. Cold, hurt, and desperate seemed preferable to being in a warm car with this unbalanced stranger.

"I don't want to be any trouble," Alexander said quietly. "I can walk the rest of the way now."

The kid looked at Alexander as though he had grown horns. "Are you kidding, dude?" he said. "Listen, I know you want to make that phone call, so once we get up to the highway, you can use my cell. It's just that it's useless until then. No reception. It's a dead zone here."

The pain behind Alexander's eyes grew. "What are you *talking* about?" he asked.

"I'm saying you can use my *phone*," the kid repeated. "Here." He pulled something out of his pocket and jabbed it in Alexander's direction. It appeared to be a rectangular metal case, smaller than a deck of cards. When the kid pushed a button, the thing lit up.

Alexander let out a startled cry and shrank against the passenger door. The sudden move made his ribs scream in agony and his hand flew to his side.

"What the hell?" the kid said. His features had twisted. His eyes were wide and his lips were curling down at the corners. He was pointing at Alexander's hands, and his face was a mask of horror. Alexander followed the direction of the kid's gaze and looked down at his own hands, lying cupped in his lap, palms up. They were dark and slick, painted in blood.

"No!" Alex cried and lifted one hand to inspect it closer. He saw that his whole sleeve was soaked in crimson. It was pooling in the small valley where his thighs met, it was trickling down his neck, and he could tell by the metallic smell that filled the car that it was not rainwater but blood that saturated his hair, his shirt, everything. He touched the spot on his torso where his ribs hurt and felt something slippery and unfamiliar there. He looked down. Glistening loops of intestine spilled through his fingers.

Alexander looked at the driver one last time. His features were still twisted as if in terror, and now there was something else—something unreal about him. About everything. The kid was beginning to shimmer like the rivulets of water that ran down the windshield. The kid was becoming transparent. Alex was passing out, he was sure of it, and he braced himself for the fall . . .

It was a long, silent fall, away from the lights of the car into the utter silence and complete darkness that he knew so well.

—

Alexander wasn't sure how long he had been walking when he came upon a cemetery. He knew it was probably only an hour or so, but it seemed like forever. *It's just an old boneyard. No big deal,* he told himself, even as he felt that familiar chill of fear run down his spine. *You know what to do.* And he did know. He simply had to put one muddy foot in front of the other and keep his eyes trained on the road. No matter what happened, he would not look into the cemetery. He would ignore the cemetery. He would walk in the rain for as long as it took, until someone came along to offer him a ride.

THE CAR OF
YOUR NIGHTMARES

One beautiful summer morning, not so long ago, a young man named Vikram set out to join his friends who were camping near Esterhazy, in southeast Saskatchewan. Vik loved getting away from the city, and this trip was going to be extra special because he had a shiny new car to drive and show off to his friends. The guys would not believe the excellent deal he had managed to negotiate with the salesman, especially as this car was a sleek little sports model and only a couple of years old.

He hadn't driven very far when he heard a woman's voice say, "Thank you for the ride." Vik slammed on the brakes. His heart pounded in his chest. *What the . . . ? Had he accidentally left the car unlocked last night? Could someone have gotten into the back seat?* He glanced at the passenger seat. It was empty. Slowly he turned to look in the back seat. It was empty. There was no one in the car with him. He blinked hard and rubbed his face. A few moments later, he decided that the voice had just been his imagination. Pretending to believe himself, Vik finally felt calm enough to continue on his way. He turned on the radio for a distraction and soon he was on the highway, singing along with tunes from the 1980s.

The traffic was light, and Vik settled in to enjoy driving his new car. When he saw a convenience store up ahead, he decided to stop for a coffee. After all, his new car had handy cupholders. He might as well take advantage.

As he walked back to his car, coffee in hand, the sun glared in his eyes. He held his free hand up to shade his vision and peered inside. The car was definitely empty. Vik breathed a sigh of relief and relaxed, sipping his coffee for a minute or two before taking to the road again.

His relaxation didn't last long. "You're kind to take me out in the country," the voice said. Vik jumped so high, he almost spilled the hot coffee all over himself. He fumbled with the door handle, trying to get away from the voice. When he finally got out, he slammed his hand down on the car roof, not knowing if he was angry or scared or both.

Something's seriously wonky here, either with me or the car, he thought.

A couple walked toward Vik and asked if he needed any help. Vik shook his head. *What could he tell them? That he was hearing voices inside his car?* He leaned against the car until his pulse rate returned to normal and then opened the car door and sat down again.

"I need to see my mother," the voice told him.

This wasn't his imagination. Something in the car was talking to him, and that something was invisible. His new ride was going back to the dealership. Now. He steeled himself for the drive back to the city and straight to the car dealer where he had bought this cursed or haunted or possessed sports car. His friends would have to camp without him this weekend.

The drive back was quiet. There were no noises from the back seat, but even so, the moment Vik parked the car on the lot, he strode into the sales office. The salesman took one look at his former customer and turned toward the back door.

"Not so fast," Vikram said loudly. "You'd better tell me who owned this car before me."

The salesman nodded meekly and led Vik into a cubicle at the far corner. He didn't want this loud and clearly unhappy customer on the sales floor.

"This is the information I think you want," the man said after scratching a few words and numbers on a scrap of paper. (This was back in the days when people were not nearly as careful as they are today about private information.)

Vik took it from him and stormed back out to his car. The address that the salesman had given him was easy to find, and at least the voice in the car wasn't speaking to him this time. He sat in the car in front of the house, trying to think about what he should say to whoever answered the door. He could hardly go charging up to a stranger's home with no clue what would come out of his mouth, or worse, tell the person that their former car talks.

He was still lost in thought when a knock on the passenger-side window startled him. *What was it with this car?* He was actually relieved when he saw an older woman standing at the curb beside his car.

"I didn't mean to startle you," she said. "You're here about the car, aren't you?"

Vik tried to speak, but no sound came out. *Yes, of course, I'm here about the car, but how does she know that?*

"I recognize this car. It was my daughter's. My husband and I bought it for her as a twenty-fifth birthday present last year. Unfortunately, she died that night. She was at a party being held in her honour. The host served shellfish. She had an allergic reaction. Her friends did what they could, but she was dead before the ambulance even got there."

"Oh, that's awful," was all Vik could manage to say.

"Did you see her ghost?"

Vik shook his head. "No, I just heard her voice. She wanted to come and see you."

The woman nodded. "That's good that you only heard her voice. Perhaps it means that her spirit's started to move on. You're the third person who's come here with the same story. Those others, though, they had seen her apparition."

"I'm so sorry for your loss," Vik muttered before the woman turned and walked into the house. He drove slowly back to the car dealership, remembering the adage that if something seems too good to be true, it probably is. No one would have sold a car like this for the price Vik paid unless they really wanted to be rid of the thing.

This time when he walked into the showroom, Vik was more focused. "You can have this car back, and I want my money back."

"We'll have to deduct a thousand dollars before we give you the refund," the salesman said. "That's not my policy. It's the boss's."

"Fine, mail me the cheque," Vik said before dropping the keys in the man's outstretched hand and walking back out into the fresh air he so badly needed.

The salesman watched him go. As Vik left, a young couple came into the showroom. "We're looking for a good used car," the woman said.

"A bit sporty would be nice, too," the man added.

The salesman smiled. "I have just the one for you two. Come with me and I'll show you this fabulous sleek little sports number. It's in almost brand-new condition."

CHILDREN OF
THE TRACKS

Not far from a campground in rural Saskatchewan, perhaps the one you're staying at right now, some train tracks cut sharply across an old country road.

One summer's evening, three teenaged sisters, Katie, Emma, and Monica, borrowed their parents' car and left the family's campsite to go exploring. The adventure was Katie's idea. She'd heard a spooky story about that railway crossing and was anxious to check it out.

Her youngest sister, Monica, complained that they didn't have to leave the campground for a scary story. After all, everyone in the family had been telling ghost stories around the campfire since their holiday began, but Katie shook her head. "It wouldn't be the same if I just tell you the story somewhere else. This is a true ghost story, and you won't believe me unless you see it for yourself."

"Right, a supposedly true ghost story. Considering there's no such thing as ghosts, this is going to have to be good," Monica complained.

"And coming way out here is supposed to make all the difference, eh?" Emma added.

Katie ignored their comments, and they all drove to a dusty old road that was really not much more than a dirt path.

"We'll have to get the car washed before we get back to the campground," Monica pointed out. "Dad'll be furious if we bring it back all covered in dust."

Katie just nodded. After bumping along on the trail for a few more metres, churning up clouds of dirt and hearing stones hit the car's undercarriage, the girls came to a slight incline and some railway tracks. Katie drove the car up the slope, only stopping when the car straddled the level tracks.

"Um—this isn't exactly safe, you know," Emma pointed out, but Katie was already out of the car and opening the trunk.

"What are you doing?" Monica asked, clearly annoyed with her sister's shenanigans.

"I'm conducting a scientific experiment."

"With Mum's bag of flour? Now when we stop to get the car washed, we'll have to buy a bag of flour too."

But Katie wasn't listening. Instead, she was sprinkling flour along the car's back bumper.

"She's lost it," Monica said to Emma, who nodded in agreement.

A moment later the oldest girl climbed back into the car. "Now I'm going to tell you the story I heard, and we'll just see if you don't think it's the freakiest one ever."

"Okay, well, we're here now, I guess," Emma acknowledged. "Go for it, but this had better be worth it."

Katie smiled that big-sister-superior smile that younger sisters all over the world know too well. Then she began to tell the tale. "A poor family once lived around here. There were seven of them living in a little shack of a house. Five kids. One evening, the father piled all of those kids into the back of his old, beaten-up pickup truck and told them they were all going to visit their grandmother in a nearby town. Trips to Grandma's house were rare, so the kids were as happy as could be.

"Their father had only driven as far as the tracks, right where we are now, when the old truck stalled. The father wasn't concerned. He knew exactly what to do to get the truck to start again. But on this particular night, it seemed that he didn't have enough time to nurse the cranky engine back to life. They were stalled on the tracks at the worst possible moment. A massive freight train was speeding toward them."

Katie had the others' attention as she continued. "He jumped out of the cab, but before he could save his kids the train was on them. The wreck was terrible. People for miles around heard the grinding scream of twisting metal. The children, though, didn't make a sound. They didn't have time. They were killed, all five of them."

"Is this really a true story?" Emma asked.

Katie nodded and continued. "A few months after the accident, a woman was driving over the tracks when she ran out of gas. She was stranded right here on the railway crossing where she knew all those children had died not long before. That alone would likely have sent a shiver running down her back, but the fact that a train was barrelling down the track toward her would absolutely have done it.

"She was about to jump and run for safety when the car suddenly started to roll. It rolled right over the tracks, down the incline on the other side, and stopped at the bottom. The train roared by, and the woman and her car were safe."

"Coincidence," Monica remarked in a tentative voice.

"Ah, but that isn't the only time that happened. About a year after that, someone had a tire blow out right on this spot and the rim wouldn't roll over the rails. Again, there was a train coming. And again, in the nick of time, the car mysteriously moved out of harm's way. It's happened plenty more times since then. Everybody around here thinks the same thing: those people were saved by the spirits of the little kids who died when the train hit them."

For a moment, none of the three sisters spoke. Finally, Emma whispered, "You think the ghosts of those five brothers and sisters are protecting everyone from meeting the same fate they did?" She seemed to be on the verge of accepting Katie's theory as the truth.

Monica was not so easily convinced, however. She just wanted them to get on their way. "Mum and Dad are going to be concerned about us if we're too late, and don't forget we still have to buy flour and get the car washed."

That comment spurred Emma to ask, "Yeah, why the flour, Katie?"

As her older sister started to reply, her voice was drowned out by the sound of a whistle. They looked down the track and saw a huge train bearing down on them.

"Start the car!" Monica and Emma yelled in unison, but Katie just sat there with a small smile on her lips.

Finally, she said quietly, "Let's stay and see what happens."

"We're going to get killed. That's what's going to happen!"

The two younger sisters jumped from the car and tried to pull Katie out as well. "The train is getting close!"

And it was. The train's headlight was getting brighter and brighter, its whistle louder and more insistent. But Katie stubbornly stayed in the car.

"Get out!" Monica and Emma screamed over and over, but their sister's face showed a look of calm confidence.

The next few moments were chaotic. The intense white headlight of the train became blindingly bright as it drew closer. The blaring whistle almost drowned out the sound of the train's grinding brakes and Katie's sisters' screams. But Katie sat quietly waiting, and soon her foolish daring and patience were rewarded. The car began to rock back and forth a little before slowly rolling forward. The vehicle cleared the tracks and rolled down the other side with only seconds to spare before the train thundered past.

The car came to a stop, and Katie climbed out, smiling. But her sisters were in no mood for pleasantries. They hugged her and yelled at her at the same time.

"I knew it," Katie bragged.

"You nearly died just now, that's what I know," Emma said.

"All this for the sake of a ghost story," Monica added.

"This is no story," Katie told them as she walked to the back of the car and pointed at the bumper. "Look at this."

Her sisters did as she said. They could hardly believe their eyes. There, on the car's bumper, in the dusting of flour, there were five distinct sets of child-sized handprints.

NEVER ALONE

Ahmed was a great guy. He was smart, friendly, and helpful, always ready to lend a friend twenty dollars or walk a neighbour's dog. He would listen to your woes if you were feeling down and even offer thoughtful, practical advice. If you were lonely, however, Ahmed would just shake his head and tell you, "Sorry, but lonely is something I've never felt."

If pushed to discuss the matter further, Ahmed would explain that he had simply never felt alone. What he didn't add was that ever since he was a kid, he always felt that someone was with him and that when he looked in a mirror, he could even see a hazy image standing just behind him. Sometimes, he could even catch a glimpse of the strange presence at the periphery of his vision.

As a little boy, Ahmed noticed that his friend, as he'd come to think of the presence, always disappeared when there was an adult nearby, so he decided not to mention anything to his parents. By the time he started elementary school, Ahmed had seen enough of his transparent companion to know that the two of them, he and the hazy outline, looked so much alike that they were pretty much identical. That made him even more determined to keep his secret to himself.

By the time he was a teenager, Ahmed began to see a certain pattern to the apparition's visits. On the evening before an important exam, for instance, his hazy self would appear. He would hover about while Ahmed studied. If he was arguing with his girlfriend or having a hard time getting along with his parents, the image was sure to visit. By the time he was an adult, he couldn't imagine his life being any other way, even though sometimes the ghost would surprise or confuse him, like the time just after college graduation when he was on his way to his first-ever job interview. He turned a corner and had to stop short to avoid crashing into a mirror. As he regained his balance, he realized that there was no mirrored surface. It was the spirit wearing an identical new navy suit, white shirt, blue tie, and dress shoes. The image faded away after a moment, but he was left with a sense of confidence and well-being. He continued on to the interview and came away with a good job.

That summer, Ahmed and a group of his friends decided to camp for a weekend at Wabamun Lake, just west of Edmonton. The getaway was great fun. Everyone swam and jet-skied and ate delicious barbecued hamburgers. That first evening, they built a campfire and sat around singing old campfire songs. When Ahmed noticed that the supply of marshmallows was running low, he slipped away to get more from the food box.

As he settled himself back into the circle, the girl sitting next to him leaned over and whispered to him, "I just saw the most amazing thing. When you stood up, it was like you divided into two people. One of you walked away, and the other stayed here by the fire. Then, just a few seconds before you returned, the other image faded away. It was remarkable."

Ahmed was taken aback. He paused for a moment and then suggested that the firelight had played tricks on the girl's eyes. "Perhaps you're right," she conceded, and he breathed a sigh of relief. He really didn't want his secret to get out. He'd come to count on his unusual advantage.

You might wonder why this double self was an advantage. Through the years that followed, if life was getting the better of him, or on the occasional night when he couldn't sleep, he would see the image out of the corner of his eye, just visible enough to be comforting. Sometimes, the figure would linger quietly for half an hour, and other times, he would only catch a fleeting glance. No wonder Ahmed never felt lonely.

Many years later, Ahmed's mother lay dying in a hospital bed. He sat with her for hours, sadly knowing that her life was quickly slipping away. It was hard for him to see her thin, pale face and listen to her raspy breathing, wondering which breath would be her last. But he couldn't bring himself to leave her, because every so often she would wake up.

After a while, it occurred to him that this could be his last chance to share his lifelong secret with his mother. "I have something to tell you," he said quietly. He then spoke at length, telling his mother about the hazy image he'd been seeing all his life, who looked exactly like him. He described the silent camaraderie that he'd enjoyed over the years, the feeling of support this had given him.

For a moment, silence hung between mother and son. Then he added, "I just wanted you to know."

His mother motioned for him to come closer to her. "There's something I've kept from you, too, son."

Ahmed clasped his mother's hand.

"You had an identical twin brother," his mother said gently. "A twin brother who died at birth."

A smile came over her face as she breathed her last breath. Ahmed watched in wonder as the presence he had felt with him all his life floated above her body, its hand outstretched. A moment later both souls were gone forever and, for the first time in his life, Ahmed felt lonely.

A MONSTROUS DAY
AT THE BEACH

Many years ago, on a sunny day in August, teenaged pals Rob and Gord drove to Thetis Lake, near Victoria on Vancouver Island. The lake was one of their favourite places to hang out, and with summer holidays drawing to a close, they were determined to make the most of the free time they had left. The weather that day was perfect, warm with just the hint of a breeze and not a cloud in the sky. Both boys were optimistic that this was going to be a day to remember. Little did they know just how memorable.

The boys told their parents that they were going for a swim, but everyone understood that the boys' main motivation for the trip to the beach was to meet girls. Their first stop was a convenience store, where they picked up some beach-worthy snacks: a large bottle of ice-cold pop and a giant-sized bag of potato chips. Then they were ready for the day.

As soon as they had parked the car, Rob and Gord ran across the hot, sandy beach toward the water, shedding clothes as they went until they were down to their bathing suits. They kept running when they reached the water and, when it was deep enough, threw themselves in. The last one into the water was definitely a rotten egg.

They swam out for a distance and then stopped to look back and assess the situation on the beach. Perfect. There were two groups of girls about their age. In typical teenaged boy fashion, Rob and Gord tried to impress the girls by dunking one another and diving from each other's shoulders. Of course, in equally typical fashion for teenaged girls, the groups on the beach didn't appear to notice.

After an hour of horseplay in the water, it was time for Rob and Gord to go ashore and break open their snacks. Maybe they would offer the girls some pop and chips. That could be a conversation starter.

Unfortunately, they didn't have time to test their plan because by the time they'd dried themselves off and started tearing into the bag of chips, both groups of girls were packing up their towels and leaving. The boys were disappointed but still determined to make the best of the afternoon. They lay on their towels, munching chips and predicting how tough their impending school year would be, especially compared to summer holidays.

They were alone on the beach now, but the sun was still high in the sky, so Rob suggested that they go back into the lake and have another swim to cool off and wash away the chip crumbs that were sticking to their damp, hot bodies. They splashed around for a while, but it just wasn't as much fun without their audience of the girls on the beach. Soon they wandered back to their towels.

"Let's not go quite yet," Gord said.

Rob agreed and pointed out that another group of girls might arrive any moment. "Let's move into the shade, though," he added. "I'm getting pretty sunburned."

They moved their towels back from the water's edge, closer to the parking lot and into the shade. Rob lay down and covered his eyes, but Gord sat staring out across the calm, still lake.

And that's when he saw it. Not far from shore, a patch of ripples disturbed the water's surface.

"Check this out," Gord said, poking his friend in the ribs. By the time Rob sat up and focused his eyes, the ripples had become a large bubble.

Rob squinted, rubbed his eyes, and looked again. Something was coming out of the water. "Let's try getting closer. It could be a huge fish."

The words were no sooner out of his mouth than a head broke the water's surface. Both boys froze as they tried to make sense of what was before them. The head rose higher. It was nearly the size of a human head, but this was no human being. At best, it was a humanoid creature, one that was standing up in the water and looking around.

Rob gasped, and Gord jumped up from the sand. He grabbed Rob's arm and tried to pull him up, but his friend was paralyzed with fear. He and the beast had locked eyes.

"Get up!" Gord screamed.

The thing that started coming out of the lake was nearly as tall as they were. It was covered with silvery scales, its hands and feet were webbed, and razor-sharp fins protruded along its head and arms. Worse, it was coming toward them—fast. Rob scrambled to his feet and chased after Gord, who was sprinting for the car, but Rob wasn't quite fast enough. The creature lunged at him, slashing deep cuts in his hand.

The boys jumped in the car, locked the doors, and sped away, with Rob holding his injured hand and squirming in pain. They drove straight to the RCMP station. Breathlessly, they told the desk sergeant what they'd seen and described how Rob's hand had been cut. The police took the boys' report seriously and began an investigation.

Three days later, the story hit the newspapers. People were horrified, especially those who knew that this wasn't the only monster associated with Vancouver Island waters. A beast resembling Scotland's Loch Ness monster was said to live in the waters of Cadboro Bay.

The Thetis Lake story was still big news when the police received a phone call from a man who thought he knew exactly what it was Gord and Rob had seen. The creature, he confessed, was nothing more than his pet lizard, which had escaped some months before. That simple explanation quelled some people's fears, but, unfortunately, it wasn't the correct explanation. Local experts were quick to declare that such a lizard could never have survived out of doors during the previous winter. Besides, the boys' description of the monster that chased them did not even vaguely resemble a lizard.

Eventually, the excitement over the sighting died down. Rob's hand healed, and the school year began. But the mystery of what that scaly, vicious beast might have been was never solved.

The story of the creature from Thetis Lake might have ended there if it hadn't been for a man named Martin, who, many years later, came forward to confess that he had visited Thetis Lake and had come away with a tale to tell.

Martin had been enjoying a solitary visit to Thetis Lake when he noticed a disturbance in the water not far from shore. Curious, he watched intently as a human-like head broke the lake's surface. For a moment, he thought it might just have been a swimmer he hadn't noticed before. But this was no ordinary swimmer: it was a scaly monster with sharp fins protruding from its head and arms, and the creature was coming toward him.

Martin ran for his car, but in his panic lost his footing and stumbled. He recovered his balance just in time. The creature was so close behind that he could smell the beast's fishy stench. Martin sprinted the last few metres to his car. Just as he slammed the door, he heard a dreadful scraping noise on the passenger-side door. He didn't feel inclined to check for damage right then. He started his car and slammed his foot on the accelerator, spraying gravel in his wake. Once he was safely on the highway, Martin slowed and pulled off to the shoulder of the road. He needed time to let his heart rate return to normal.

It wasn't until he had calmed down and finished his drive home that he thought to check the side of his car. Chills of fear shot down his back when he saw a deep gouge in the door. Five marks lined the door, with patches of fishy scales embedded in the car's paint. No wonder it took him years before he was able to speak of his encounter at Thetis Lake.

If by chance you're thinking that Gord and Rob's and Martin's reports are merely figments of overactive imaginations, then be sure to check the details in Haden Blackman's book, *The Field Guide to North American Monsters* or, perhaps even more convincingly, listen to Indigenous legends that describe the Thetis Lake Monster exactly as these eyewitnesses have recorded.

A day at the beach, anyone?

DEAD AT THE DINER

When his sons were children, Rakeesh took them camping every year, but now that they were older, it was difficult to find a time when all of them could get away. Finally, the three managed to get their summer holidays booked for the same week, so they made arrangements for a camping trip. When the date arrived, they wasted no time in hitting the road. They had packed the night before so they could get on their way to Manipogo Park on Lake Manitoba as soon as they possibly could.

Before they had gone very far, though, they realized they should have packed sandwiches for the trip. But they hadn't, so instead, they pulled over at the first roadside diner they came to.

Nikhil walked into the restaurant first. He'd only taken a few steps inside when he stopped and blinked several times before turning to his father and brother, Vinay.

"This place is so dark, I can hardly see," he complained.

"The food smells good, though," his father said as he guided them to a booth. In silence, they each grabbed a greasy menu from between the salt and pepper shakers.

Moments later, a young waiter approached their table. "Are you folks ready to order?" he asked with obvious disinterest.

Rakeesh turned to Vinay. "Decided on anything yet, son?"

"Not yet," Vin said and looked across the table at his brother, who seemed to be staring off into space. "Nik, you order first."

There was no reply.

"Nikhil, I said, you go first. What are you going to have?"

Rakeesh glanced from one son to the other. Vin looked mildly annoyed, which wasn't unusual when he was with his brother, but Nikhil looked terrible. Beads of sweat dotted his forehead, he was pale, and his eyes were glassy. Was he getting a migraine? It had been years since he had endured one of those, but in his teens, he had been tormented by headaches, and his father had become familiar with the look that would come over him just before the pain hit. Everyone had optimistically decided that he had outgrown them. Perhaps everyone had been wrong.

"Nik!" The father's concern for his younger son put such an edge in his voice that Vin was taken aback. Their father usually didn't sound stern like that—normally, he was a pretty easygoing guy.

"Huh?" Nikhil looked at his father and brother. "I can't even think about food. Look at that guy over there, the one at the corner table with the red sweatshirt on. He's freaky, man. Worse than freaky."

Vin followed his younger brother's gaze to a darkened table in the corner of the restaurant, where a heavy-set man wearing an oversized red sweatshirt sat by himself. The guy certainly wasn't eye candy, but calling him "freaky" was a bit much. Vin glanced at his father, whose eyebrows were raised. No one spoke.

"I'll give you a couple more minutes, then," the waiter said and shuffled away.

"Dad, do something!" Nikhil urged in a stage whisper.

"What? Do something about what?" Rakeesh asked, sounding confused.

"About that guy being in here! It's disgraceful. A dead guy should *not* be in a restaurant." Nik's voice was shrill, verging on panic.

"A dead guy?" his father asked.

Vin shoved his cutlery aside. He hadn't eaten since early morning and he was getting impatient. "Knock it off, stupid, and just order your food. I'm hungry."

"But how can you be hungry when you can look at that . . . that . . . *thing?*"

Rakeesh sighed. This was not a good start to their camping trip. "Nik, are you all right? If you're not, please say so, but if you're okay, then either tell us what we're supposed to be seeing or drop the nonsense."

Nikhil put the palms of his hands on the table and spoke slowly. "The guy in the corner over there can't be alive. They must have propped him up somehow. Look at him. His shirt is all ripped and filthy. He's dead! How could they let anyone bring him in here? I'm calling the police."

Rakeesh looked toward the corner table and then back at his son. He put his hand on Nikhil's arm. "It's just the dim lighting over there in the corner—too many shadows. It's too dark in the whole place, if you ask me, but who cares? The guy's getting up to leave anyway."

Vin nodded. "Yeah, the dude's going, Nik, so snap out of it. Come on, let's just order our lunch, okay? We need to get back on the road, or we'll be pitching our tent in the dark."

Nikhil took a deep breath and muttered, "Yeah, I guess. I'll just have a burger, but would you order for me? I'm going to the men's room to splash some water on my face."

After Nikhil had walked away, Rakeesh held up his hand to signal the waiter. Just then a tremendous thump reverberated through the restaurant. Diners, including Rakeesh and Vin, jumped up from their tables and ran to the window.

The guy who had been sitting at the corner table had walked out onto the highway and directly into the path of a semi-trailer. His red-sweatshirted, heavy-set body had flown like a rag doll and landed on the road in a crumpled, lifeless heap.

Rakeesh turned to his son. "Vin, get Nikhil. Find a back door and take him out that way. I'll bring the car around. We're getting out of here, *now!*"

LITTLE GIRL LOST

Warren owned a large tract of land in east-central Saskatchewan. He had bought it decades ago and had turned the property into an excellent income investment by creating a campground with all the bells and whistles. Every site had all the hookups campers needed, and the shower and laundry facilities he offered were second to none. But it wasn't as though this campground was a recipe for easy money; Warren worked hard to keep his clientele happy, and he succeeded. As a result, he hosted the same groups of campers year after year and turned a tidy profit.

After each busy summer, though, he was always anxious to go back to the isolated living that he preferred. One of the reasons he had originally chosen to live where he did was that it was not easily accessible. No one would stumble upon the place "accidentally," since it was well off the beaten path and the driveway was nearly a kilometre long.

And so it was that Warren was somewhat annoyed on a rainy October evening when he heard knocking at his front door.

"Who the dickens would be pounding on my door at this time of night?" he grumbled and, for a moment, debated not answering the door. He was watching a rerun of *Law and Order*, and it was one of his favourite episodes. But he was a curious man by nature, and so, after a moment's thought, he eased himself out of his tattered recliner.

"What?" he shouted as he threw open the heavy wooden door. For a moment, it looked as though no one was there. Then he looked down and saw a little girl, not much more than a metre tall, standing on the porch, shivering in the cold, rainy night, staring up at him with pleading eyes.

"Who are you? What are you doing here?" he barked at the child.

"I live here," the tiny waif replied.

"You most certainly do not live here. I live here!"

"But I do live here—in the orphanage." The child's voice was as thin as she was.

"Don't be ridiculous, girl. This isn't an orphanage. This is my home. Now away with you and don't be bothering me again," Warren said firmly.

"I stayed out for a long time, as long as I could. I was scared to come back because I was afraid I'd get into trouble. I just wanted to go for a walk by myself. I went out by the back door without anyone seeing me, but I got so cold and lost."

Warren stared at the child. This must be a joke. He knew that there had been a children's home in the area, but that had been many years ago. Orphanages had been a thing of the past for decades. Who did this skinny little brat think she was trying to fool? The kid was putting him in a bad spot. He couldn't leave a child out there alone at night. He would have to do something, but what?

"There's not much to you, is there? No wonder you're cold. You'd just better not be playing a trick on me, you little urchin," Warren said sternly. "Come in here where it's warmer until we get this sorted out."

The child nodded solemnly and stepped into the house. As she did, her image softened.

"You just stay here in the hall," Warren instructed as he headed for the phone. "I'm going to call the police. They'll know what to do with you."

The child didn't answer. Warren turned back toward the little girl and watched in terror as the child's image began to break up into tiny points of light until her body was a mere echo of itself, a glistening column of tiny flickering lights that vanished before his eyes.

Warren leaned up against the wall to keep himself on his feet. He rubbed his eyes and told himself he'd fallen asleep during the television show and had dreamed the whole bizarre event. For a moment, he tried to convince himself. Then he looked down at the floor where the little girl's spirit had stood. There, before his eyes, were two tiny footprints in a puddle of rainwater.

Warren eased his way back into his recliner, but the show he had been watching had finished. He shook his head and wondered if next summer he might have the courage to tell his campers about his encounter with the lost little ghost girl from so long ago.

JOKER'S WILD

Grant and Jessie and their friends, Sean and Danielle, were driving home after a week of camping in Northern Manitoba.

"Thanks for taking us along," Sean said to Grant, who was driving his truck, which was fitted out with a camper in the truck bed.

"Sorry you and Danielle are crammed into the crew cab back there," Grant replied. "But we'll stop every now and then to stretch our legs."

The words were no sooner out of his mouth than Sean spotted a sign advertising a restaurant and pub up ahead. "Let's pull in there," he suggested.

"That place is as old as the hills," Jessie said. "My grandfather and his friends used to stop here on road trips. It was called Joker's Wild. The dining room was at the back. It was called the King's Table. My grandfather talked about it a lot. It's funny, the things you remember from childhood. He told me that the owner's name was Joe and that occasionally he'd let Grandpa and his friends play poker at a table way back in a darkened corner of the pub."

Grant took his eyes away from the road for a moment and looked over at Jessie. "We stopped there last year, don't you remember? The place was a dump."

"Well, sorry, but I have to use the washroom, so I think we'd better stop," Danielle said, with some urgency.

A few minutes later, Grant obligingly pulled off into the parking lot. "The parking lot looks better than it did last year. Maybe they've cleaned up the place."

All four tired campers trooped into the old log building. Inside, the place was as neat and clean and inviting as could be. "Wow," Grant exclaimed. "Someone's really put a lot of work into this place since we were here before. Let's sit down and have a bite to eat."

The other three nodded in agreement, and soon a young man came to their table with menus and tall glasses of ice water.

"I'll bet the days of letting people play poker in here are long gone," Jessie commented.

"No doubt, but check it out. The new owner's kept the original sign," Sean said, pointing to a spot above the kitchen door.

The others turned to admire the aged plank of wood with faded red paint spelling out JOKER'S WILD across the top; below, in black paint, were the words KING'S TABLE.

They were all ravenous, so they quickly opened their menus and silently perused the selections. Then Jessie set her menu down on the table. "We're in a pub, so let's have pub grub. At least for the appetizer."

Her suggestion was popular with everyone in the group, and the nachos were the best they'd ever eaten.

"Yum, that was delicious," Sean said, wiping his fingers on a large paper napkin.

Danielle nodded. "Good food, definitely. I hope the new owner does well, especially since he's gone to so much trouble to respect the building's history, like keeping that old sign and the original name."

"I think it's bad luck to change a name," Jessie said. "Especially here."

"Why's that?" Danielle asked.

Jessie continued, "My grandfather told me that the man who started this business had quite an ego. He even subtly named the place after himself. His name was Joe King, so that's why the pub is called Joker's Wild and the restaurant is called King's Table."

Danielle laughed. "That was pretty darned clever!"

"There's quite a story about the old sign, too."

"Well, we're here, and you've told us this much already, so you'd better tell us about the sign." Grant smiled and took a sip of his drink. This was a tale he had heard many times from members of Jessie's family.

"Remember I said that old Joe had quite an ego? Well, when he had that sign painted, he had a picture of himself painted in the centre of it."

"He was vain, wasn't he?" Danielle said as she put on her jacket, which was on the seat beside her. When Sean looked at her questioningly, she added, "I'm cold. We must be sitting under an air conditioning outlet."

Jessie nodded. "After Joe died, his friends held a wake for him right here in the pub. It was a bad night—rainy and cold—but my grandfather and his buddies came to pay their respects. They decided it would be fitting to have a quick round of poker in honour of their deceased friend. My grandfather swears that as the cards were dealt, he looked up and saw Joe—well, his spirit, at least—drenched with rain, standing by the table. Grandpa didn't say anything to anyone because he didn't want his friends to think he was crazy, but the apparition upset him so much that he left the wake right away. It was teeming down rain by then, just a miserable night. As my grandfather was walking to his truck, he looked back toward the pub to see if anyone else was leaving and might need a drive home. As he did, he noticed something very strange about the sign."

Danielle hugged her jacket around herself.

Jessie lowered her voice. "The picture of Joe on the sign had just disappeared."

"That's just a tall tale, a bunch of hokum your grandfather made up to . . . " Sean started to say dismissively.

A sudden blast of frigid air silenced him.

Anger flushed Jessie's face. She hated that Sean had disrespected her family's legend. She reached for her menu again. Two playing cards fell from inside the menu—a joker and a king.

She shivered as the air in the room turned colder still.

THE THING
IN THE CLOSET

The cabin sat at the edge of a lake in central British Columbia. For ten months each year, I had the place to myself. July and August, however, were horrendous for me. Honestly, those months were so bad that, for the most part, I just stayed crouched in the very back of the bedroom closet, making myself as small as I possibly could. Whenever I heard them moving, I barely dared to breathe—from fear, of course, but also because of the awful smell.

I'd hear one of them moving around in the main part of the bedroom. I was helpless. There was absolutely no way of predicting when it would stop prowling and settle. Until it did, there was nothing I could do but wait. The stress was unbearable. It was almost impossible to stay still, yet my very existence depended on remaining undetected.

Finally, the strip of light across the bottom of the closet door disappeared. It was safe. I burst from my hiding place. But it saw me! It screamed so loud that another one came running. Just in time, I slunk back to the closet where I'd been hiding and made myself as small as I could.

"Gilbert, you make enough noise to wake the dead. When are you going to get over this? There is nothing hiding in the back of your closet."

I receded even farther to the back corner of the closet and fought to remain still. I couldn't take any chances for, you see, I'd heard tales of things like me who'd been seen—and those stories *never* ended well at all.

THE GIRL
ON THE BRIDGE

Once upon a time, Western Canada was dotted with enormous wooden trestle bridges that carried trains across the prairie's streams and valleys. The bridges were built when lumber was plentiful and not nearly as expensive as it is now. They were also built to last, and that's why many of them are still standing—giant monuments to the pioneers' ingenuity.

Often, at the base of a trestle bridge, you would find the area's favourite swimming hole, and that was certainly the case with a beautiful old bridge that still stands just north of Edmonton and just east of a popular campground. Many people say that bridge is haunted, and the ghost is said to be the spirit of a young woman.

Local legend has it that the young woman and her boyfriend had arranged to meet at the bridge for a midnight swim. The sky was clear that night, and there was a beautiful full moon. The girl had put her bathing suit on under her clothes and told her parents she was going to visit a friend. Then she headed straight to the bridge. Her boyfriend wasn't there when she arrived, but she couldn't resist the cool water. She went for a swim by herself.

Swimming alone is never a good idea, and it certainly wasn't for that girl on that night. No one knows whether or not her boyfriend ever showed up, but we do know that the girl's lifeless body was found the next day on the embankment.

Even now, it is said that when the sky is clear and the moon is full, you can see the girl's ghost on the old trestle bridge. Don't be afraid to stare if you should happen to see her presence. She won't be offended. She doesn't seem to be aware of today's surroundings at all. Her apparition is frozen in time, wearing her old-fashioned bathing suit.

Now, you might wonder how a person could tell whether the image they're seeing is a ghost or, perhaps, a real flesh-and-blood girl who's simply gone for a swim. Apparently, detecting the difference is quite easy, because the ghost will stare at you—with empty eye sockets.

BREAKING UP
CAN BE DEADLY

"You have to be kidding me!"

Megan was aghast when she saw Garth standing at the campground gate. He had ruined her entire summer by breaking up with her in June, right at the end of the school year. Now, just before school was due to start again, there he was again. Worse, he looked a total wreck. If he was hoping to get back in her good books, he could at least have made himself look presentable. As it was, his hair was caked with mud, his shirt was ripped, and his jeans weren't just dirty, they were filthy.

Anger flooded through Megan's veins. "I hope you're not so stupid as to think I might be interested in getting back together with you."

Garth didn't reply. He didn't even move. As a matter of fact, he was still standing mutely, staring at Megan when she turned from the gate and ran back to the campsite where she and her parents and sisters were vacationing. Thankful that the rest of the family had apparently gone to the beach, she threw herself on her sleeping bag and sobbed.

An hour later, just as her sobs were easing, Megan's mother came into the tent. The heartbroken, angry girl pretended she was asleep when her mother came to her side.

"Later, let's go for a stroll on the beach," her mother said quietly. Megan really just wanted to stay quietly by herself. But maybe Megan's mom thought a walk along St. Ambroise Beach, one of the most beautiful beaches in Manitoba, would lift Megan's spirits.

Megan hadn't told her parents when Garth had broken up with her. It was just easier that way. They had never completely approved of her relationship with him, and if they'd noticed that he hadn't been around all summer, they certainly hadn't said anything about it.

Yes, a walk would give Megan a chance to tell her mother everything, including Garth's visit today.

When she heard her mother leave the tent, Megan sat up in her sleeping bag. Her eyes were still swollen and red from crying, but she could explain that to her mother as they walked along the beach and gazed out at beautiful Lake Manitoba.

She let herself out of the tent and looked around for her mother. "A walk on the beach sounds good, Mom," Megan said when she finally spotted her sitting on a log by the firepit, deep in thought. "It'll give us a chance to talk. There's something I've been meaning to tell you."

"Can it wait a few moments, dear? There's something *I* need to tell *you*." Her mother's voice sounded odd, strained somehow. It had a brittle edge to it. Megan wondered briefly if there was something wrong with one of her grandparents.

"I'm sure you knew that your father and I didn't much like Garth or the amount of time you were spending with him during the school year," said her mother. "We were actually afraid you'd want to spend every waking moment with him this summer, so I have to tell you we were relieved that he hasn't been around these last couple of months."

"Actually, that's exactly what I wanted to talk to you about," Megan interjected.

"Let me finish, dear," her mother continued. "I've just had a phone call from Garth's mother. Their family was camping, but they came home early. It seems there's been a terrible tragedy, Megan. Some hikers found Garth at the bottom of a hill. Well, they found his remains, that is. As best as anyone could tell, he'd fallen and died instantly."

Megan stopped in her tracks. The dishevelled image at the campground gate must have been Garth's ghost. He'd come to see her one last time.

DEAD TIRED

Jim knew he should have left Tunnel Mountain campground, near Banff, hours before he did. But everyone had been having so much fun sitting around the campfire, talking and telling stories and singing old camp songs. He just hadn't been able to tear himself away sooner. Now, though, he would pay the price for his lack of willpower by having to drive home in the dark when he was dead tired. Worse still, he had to get up early for work the next day. *When will I learn?* Jim thought and shook his head.

A thick layer of clouds covered the stars and the moon that might have lit his way, and there were no streetlights on the roads ahead. He would really have to pay attention. Jim opened the car windows so that the cool night air would help keep him alert while he was driving. Then, just to be extra safe, he tuned the radio to a hard-rock station and cranked up the volume. *That ought to do it*, he thought. He looked forward to getting home to Calgary. At least he wouldn't have any traffic to contend with. He hadn't seen another car or truck on the road since he'd driven through the park gates. *Clearly*, he thought, *every other soul in the world is wiser than I am.*

Jim had not put more than ten kilometres between him and the campground when the noise of the hard-rock radio station began to get on his nerves. The music wasn't so bad, but the disc jockey was an idiot. He tried a classic-rock station, but those tunes were way too mellow to keep him awake. He squirmed in the seat. His right leg was cramped from pressing on the accelerator, and his eyes were stinging from tiredness and the strain of trying to see the road ahead. This was going to be a miserable drive. He vowed he would never again do anything this stupid. He had lots of seniority at work: if he'd taken Monday off, he could have driven home comfortably in the morning.

Well, he hadn't, so his options were severely limited. He could either keep driving or pull over and sleep for a while, but the temptation to get home to his own bed was too great, so Jim kept going. He still hadn't seen another vehicle on the road.

Keeping the windows open no longer seemed to be a wise choice. It was cold in the car, and the constant wind was making his ears ring. *I've never been this uncomfortable in my entire life*, he thought. Even his fingers felt stiff on the wheel. He turned on the car's heater and soon felt much more comfortable. The warm air was so welcome, and even the whirl of the heater fan's motor felt companionable somehow.

Then, all the discomfort and stress he'd been feeling eased away, and it seemed to Jim that he was exactly where he wanted to be—at home in bed. Except that he wasn't. He'd fallen asleep at the wheel, and he stayed asleep until his car hit the guardrail on the opposite side of the road. Seconds later, he was unconscious again, knocked out cold, while his car careened end over end before plunging to land upside down in a creek below.

When Jim came to, he had no idea where he was or what had happened. He only knew that somehow he had to get out of the car, but try as he might, he couldn't get the seatbelt undone. "Help me!" he screamed uselessly inside the wrecked car. That futile cry for help was all he could manage before he passed out again.

Sometime later, an unfamiliar noise penetrated his fogged brain. Jim opened his eyes wide enough to see that an old lady wearing big glasses was standing by the car and was tapping on the window with an oversized red-and-white ring. He blinked and looked again. She looked like someone from an old movie. *I have to be imagining this. Or worse. Maybe I'm already dead!* No, he had to be alive. He was breathing, and the elderly, old-fashioned-looking lady had to be real, because she was talking to him. Had she seen his car go off the road and then climbed down through the bush to help him? Jim's trauma-addled brain accepted that premise.

"You can do it, Jimmy," she urged him.

If an old lady could climb down here, then surely he could at least get himself out of the car. But no matter how hard he tried, he couldn't free himself from the tangled seatbelt.

"You can do it, Jimmy," the woman urged again.

Jimmy? Who calls me Jimmy? And how does she know my name anyway?

He struggled with the seatbelt again, but the pain in his right arm was so bad that he couldn't get his fingers to work. There wasn't any question that he had broken some bones.

"You can do it, Jimmy," she repeated.

Slowly, painfully, he reached around with his left hand and managed to undo the buckle.

"You did it!" the woman exclaimed. "Now open the door. You can do it."

The car was lying on its left side, but after several moments of struggling, he managed to release the lock. No matter how hard he tried, though, he couldn't push it open.

"You can do it, Jimmy. You can do it," said the old woman again.

Jim held his breath and gave the door the hardest push he could. It opened just enough to let him squeeze out of the car and onto the bank of the small creek. He looked around. It took him a minute to find his bearings. Where was the old lady? She was nowhere to be seen. *She must've climbed back up to the road,* he thought, as he tried to scramble away from the car, now suddenly clear-headed enough to realize that the wreck could burst into flames any second. He began clawing his way up the slope with one hand, his injured right arm dragging uselessly at his side.

"You can do it, Jimmy." He looked up and saw the old lady standing a few metres away from him at the road edge. Agonizingly slowly, he crawled toward her. He barely reached the roadside before he passed out again.

The next thing Jim knew, a man was shaking his shoulder and talking to him. "I've called for help, so just stay with us, fella. Help is on the way." Jim tried to nod at the man and then closed his eyes and drifted away into oblivion again until flashing red lights disturbed his peaceful unconsciousness.

Jim could hear people talking. The man was telling the two people in uniforms, "I wouldn't have noticed him here at the side of the road if there hadn't been an old woman with him. She flagged me down. I don't know where she went after that."

Jim could feel himself being lifted onto a stretcher and put into some kind of vehicle. Then he heard a siren, its scream unrelenting and close to him until he finally realized that he was in the back of an ambulance on the way to the hospital. Once again, he sank into blissful oblivion.

Before the ambulance had driven off, one of the medics turned to the stranger and said, "You've done your good deed for the day by phoning us and waiting with him. He'd have been a goner if he'd stayed at the side of the road much longer."

"It wasn't just me. That old woman must have been the one who helped him up the hill. She was wearing a big, honkin' red-and-white ring and the craziest glasses I've ever seen."

—

The next voice Jim heard was familiar. "Jim, it's Dad. Wake up." He opened his eyes, and sure enough, there was his father standing beside him as he lay on a gurney in a hospital corridor.

"You've been in an accident, Jim, but the doctors say you'll be all right," his father assured him as he gave him a sip of water from a bottle with a straw protruding from it. The drink was so welcome. It meant he'd lived through the ordeal.

Feeling secure in the knowledge that he was still alive, Jim fell asleep. When he woke up, his right arm was in a cast from wrist to shoulder and his head pounded painfully, but he was propped up in the bed and aware of what was going on around him. His parents and his brother were all there at his bedside.

"What happened?" Jim asked.

"Your car went over a cliff. You must've climbed up to the road. A driver going in the other direction noticed you," his older brother explained.

"Was the driver an old woman?"

"No, it was a man. He called for the ambulance."

"But there was an elderly woman with me the whole time," Jim said, his voice still weak from the trauma.

"It's odd that you should say that," his father said in a quiet voice. "The man who found you told the police that an elderly lady had flagged him down but that once he'd called for help she disappeared."

Jim nodded. "She was definitely there. She knocked on the car window with this crazy big ring, and she was wearing old-fashioned cat-eye glasses. She kept calling me Jimmy. How would some passerby have known my name, and who calls me Jimmy?"

Jim's family silently stared at their loved one in the hospital bed. His father cleared his throat before he spoke. "The driver gave the same description. I've had some time to think about this, and I know exactly who it was that came to you and stayed with you until help arrived. That was your grandmother, Jim. She died before you were two years old. She loved costume jewellery, and her glasses were from the sixties."

Jim's mother suddenly made the connection, too, and added that when the young man was a baby, just learning to walk, his grandmother always encouraged him by saying, "You can do it, Jimmy."

"She was right then, and she was right yesterday," said his mom.

It took a while for the significance of his encounter to resonate fully in Jim's brain, but when it did, he never looked at life in quite the same way, and he certainly never again drove at night when he was dead tired.

ONE LAST STORY

The Bouchard family loved to camp in the summer. Over the years, they had stayed in campgrounds from the eastern edge of Manitoba to the western edge of Vancouver Island, but they all agreed that this year's campground, in rural Saskatchewan, was the best one they'd ever stayed at. The place had everything: a gorgeous lake, canoes and rowboats, fishing gear, hiking trails, a circle of excellent campsites, and, best of all, every evening at twilight a storyteller came to the circle of trailers, RVs, and tents to tell scary tales. Everyone agreed that he was a wonderful storyteller.

But now, sadly, summer was nearly over. People were packing up and getting ready to go back to the city. Of course, the kids were especially sad because the end of August also meant that school was about to start again for another year. On that last evening, everyone stayed around the main campfire later than usual. The storyteller had spun them a yarn about a crazed maniac being in the back seat of a young woman's car. It was an old tale, but the narrator still managed to make it scary.

When the story was finished, the man said goodbye to his summer friends, but the group weren't ready to let him go. "Please tell us one last story," they begged.

"What would you like to hear?" he asked.

"Something scary," a teenager suggested, while a little girl called out that she'd like a story with some magic in it.

"You've never told us a werewolf story," someone in the back noted.

The storyteller shook his head and told them he only knew one more story and that he was sure they wouldn't want to hear it.

Naturally, the entire group, children and adults alike, begged him to tell the tale.

"Not this one," he said firmly. "It's too scary."

The campers all sagged in disappointment and began tidying up the blankets they'd been sitting on and the empty bags of marshmallows that were lying around.

Then a woman near the edge of the circle asked, "Is it a vampire story?"

A boy across from her suggested the untold story was about Freddy Krueger, but the storyteller just shook his head.

When a little girl tugged on his sleeve pleading for one more story, he told her, "Trust me. You do not want to hear this story." As he spoke, his voice sounded odd, much deeper than it had before and a bit shivery. When he stood up, he seemed much taller than before, somehow.

"Okay, if you're not going to tell it to us, will you at least tell us why?" a young woman asked.

The man slowly turned his back to the crowd. Then he turned around again to face them. Their excellent storyteller had transformed into something that was loathsome beyond description, horrifying beyond anything that they had ever seen in their vivid imaginations.

"You don't want to hear my last story," he said in a dreadful, raspy voice. "Because no one knows the ending."

With that, the storyteller nodded and slowly turned away from the fire again. When he turned back toward them, he had changed yet again—into a monster with massive jaws, open as if to attack the campers. He bellowed menacingly at the frightened campers, and then, in an instant, he was gone. All that was left was a puff of smoke and a small clump of singed fur.

The fire had burned itself out before any of the campers dared to move. Then, one by one in the dark silence, the adults hurried their children off to bed and no one said a word about what had just happened—ever.

AFTERWORD

Ahhh, there you are, my extra-curious campers. You're the
ones who are interested in knowing which of the campfire stories in this book are based on actual events. Well, you've come to
the right place. These are the five true stories that I have dramatized for *Ghostly Campfire Stories of Western Canada:*

The Graveyard of the Pacific

While the characters Troy and Mark are figments of my imagination, the sinking of the ship *Valencia* was an actual event, a
tragedy of mammoth proportions. The iron-hulled steamer met
her demise in a storm that tossed it like a child's toy against the
rocky coastline of Vancouver Island in January 1906. The wreck
of the *Valencia* still holds the tragic distinction of being the
worst shipwreck in that area, which has earned itself the equally
tragic moniker, the Graveyard of the Pacific.

Although it's difficult now to determine an accurate tally of
the number of lives lost in the sinking of the *Valencia*, we know
for certain that at least 130 souls perished that terrible night and
that there were only a handful of survivors.

We also know that over the years, credible witnesses have seen the image of the *Valencia,* complete with apparitions of the ship's terrified passengers and crew clinging to the riggings and screaming for help as the ghost of that long-lost ship is battered by winds and waves, swamping her deck into eternity.

The West Coast Trail that we know today started out as the Dominion Lifesaving Trail. It was created in 1907 in response to the wreck of the *Valencia* and was intended as a way for potential rescuers to get to ships in trouble and for survivors of shipwrecks to get to help.

Even the sighting of the *Valencia*'s lifeboat, with its skeletal occupants, is a documented report. Apparently, an unusually low tide revealed the entrance to a cave that at normal tide is submerged. On that day, a group of fishermen reported that they had drifted into the cave's mouth and that is where they saw the remains of the *Valencia*'s lifeboat. Inside the small boat were eight skeletons. No doubt the small craft had been washed in by waves breaking hard against the shore at high tide.

The Valencia Hotel in San Francisco also existed and was destroyed by the earthquake that devastated that city on April 18, 1906, coincidentally less than four months after the steamship *Valencia* sank. I have no idea, though, whether or not any of the ill-fated ship's crew had actually been staying there. We do know, however, that clearly, neither the hotel nor the ship were strong enough to withstand the natural forces pitted against them.

An Encounter with the Past

Every word of this story is true! Susan went on to become a teacher at a special school in Edmonton. I visited that school often to do readings for the students and talk to them about the stories I'd collected. Susan approached me after one of these sessions and told me about the experience she'd had while driving through the Crowsnest Pass from her home in Lethbridge on her way to her summer job in the southern interior of British Columbia.

The Vampire

This is a true story, but I have taken liberties with the location. For the full account of the Croglin Grange vampire, see Jo-Anne Christensen's *Victorian Ghost Stories*.

Wampohama

Wampohama, who was also known as Mother Damnable, was a Huron woman who lived hundreds of years ago on land that we now know as Winnipeg. She was gifted with the ability to foretell the future, and her prophecies were published as a small book entitled *A Short Account of the Old Indian Witch, Wampohama: Better Known to the Early Settlers as Mother Damnable, Together with her Extraordinary Prophecies, Already Partially Fulfilled, Concerning the Future Destinies of What Are Now Winnipeg, Manitoba, and the Great North-West.* That handle would certainly never get past a publisher's marketing department today!

One of Wampohama's predictions was that Western Canada would remain "wild and unpopulated for two hundred years [but] then it shall give food to the eastern tribes." By the early 1900s, Western Canada began producing wheat that still feeds the eastern provinces.

Although the book is no longer in print, you can find references to it in John Robert Colombo's book *Mysterious Canada: Strange Sights, Extraordinary Events, and Peculiar Places*, and in Jo-Anne Christensen's *Ghosts, Werewolves, Witches and Vampires* (see bibliography for details).

A Monstrous Day at the Beach

The story of the creature in Thetis Lake is also true! For generations, the Coast Salish who lived in the area spoke in careful tones when they related the legend of the monster in that lake.

The story of the teenaged boys' encounter with the humanoid creature is a matter of police record and was reported in the *Victoria Daily Times* on August 22, 1972. Martin's misadventure with the beast occurred more recently, on November 1, 2011. Don't you just wonder if he still drives the same vehicle, the one with the monstrous scratches on the door?

ACKNOWLEDGEMENTS

Thanks to everyone at Heritage House for sharing their talents to improve my work, and special thanks to Rodger Touchie for suggesting this second volume as a follow-up to *Campfire Stories of Western Canada*. Thanks to Lara Kordic, Leslie Kenny, the ever-patient and skilled editor Karla Decker, designer Jacqui Thomas, proofreader Jesmine Cham, and editorial coordinator Lenore Hietkamp, and to my dear friend, Jo-Anne Christensen, for editorial guidance.

My sincere thanks to booksellers. Please know you are appreciated.

Much love and special thanks always to my ever-growing family.

SUGGESTED READING

Blackman, Haden W. *Field Guide to North American Monsters: Everything You Need to Know About Encountering Over One Hundred Terrifying Creatures in the Wild.* New York: Three Rivers Press, 1998.

Christensen, Jo-Anne. *Ghosts, Werewolves, Witches and Vampires.* Edmonton: Lone Pine Publishing, Edmonton, 2001.

———. *Victorian Ghost Stories.* Edmonton: Ghost House Books, 2004.

Colombo, John Robert. *Mysterious Canada: Strange Sights, Extraordinary Events, and Peculiar Places.* Toronto: Doubleday Canada, 1988.

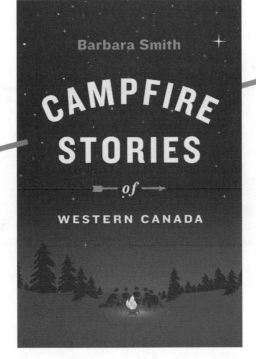

Barbara Smith

CAMPFIRE STORIES

of

WESTERN CANADA

978-1-77203-112-6

Available where all fine books are sold.

heritagehouse.ca

ABOUT THE AUTHOR

Barbara Smith is the author of over thirty books, including *Campfire Stories of Western Canada, The Famous Five, The Valiant Nellie McClung, Hoaxes and Hexes, The Mad Trapper,* and perennial bestsellers *Ghost Stories of Alberta, Ghost Stories and Mysterious Creatures of British Columbia,* and *Ghost Stories of the Rocky Mountains.*